The Great
ScrumMaster

The Great ScrumMaster

#ScrumMasterWay

Zuzana Šochová

♦♦Addison-Wesley

Boston • Columbus • Indianapolis • New York • San Francisco • Amsterdam • Cape Town
Dubai • London • Madrid • Milan • Munich • Paris • Montreal • Toronto • Delhi • Mexico City
São Paulo • Sydney • Hong Kong • Seoul • Singapore • Taipei • Tokyo

For information about buying this title in bulk quantities, or for special sales opportunities (which may include electronic versions; custom cover designs; and content particular to your business, training goals, marketing focus, or branding interests), please contact our corporate sales department at corpsales@pearsoned.com or (800) 382-3419.

For government sales inquiries, please contact governmentsales@pearsoned.com.

For questions about sales outside the U.S., please contact intlcs@pearson.com.

Visit us on the Web: informit.com/aw

Library of Congress Control Number: 2016957432

ISBN-13: 978-0-13-465711-0
ISBN-10: 0-13-465711-X

6 2020

For all ScrumMasters, Agile coaches, and leaders

CONTENTS

FOREWORD

Zuzana Šochová—Zuzi—is the author of a new book on the #ScrumMasterWay. She is also the heart and soul of the Agile Prague Conference, which is where I had the great fortune to meet her several years ago. A beautiful lady in a beautiful city. As its name suggests, this is a guidebook along the path, the way, for ScrumMasters and Agile coaches.

The book covers a lot. You'll find thumbnail sketches of many valuable approaches as well as useful examples based on hard-earned real experience. This makes this a good reference for techniques after you have been through the book.

Zuzi reads a lot. Her talks are entertaining and informative as she brings what she has read to the attention of the rest of the community. Zuzi also has the Agile mindset, and her message is to encourage readers to be the same. Take small steps, and even when discouraged, keep moving forward. This sounds a lot like the recommendations in *Fearless Change* and *More Fearless Change*! As I am deeply interested in change, I echo the approach Zuzi takes. Instead of the grand plans most organizations have for overnight upheaval and a deadline—"We will be agile by the end of 2016"—successful change is built around small steps and learning. In *Fearless Change*, we describe a "Learning Cycle." Take a small step. Stop. Make time for reflection and learning. Based on small successes, take the next small step. Of course, we'd like to reach a tipping point, when the change takes on a life of its own and things begin to be easier, but we can't count on that! The best approach is based on small experiments.

You will love the sketches in Zuzi's book! Research shows we learn from images. In fact, words themselves are recognized by the brain as images. Zuzi's imaginative drawings are the perfect addition to the material.

The book offers a chance for reflection and evaluation of strengths and areas that need improvement—this is perhaps the most important part of the book. We know it's difficult to understand ourselves. Without some planned time-outs, we have no hope of improvement. It won't happen by accident. Research has shown that just a few minutes each day looking back on what worked well and what should be improved can show real benefit over time.

I really like her discussion of the Cynefin framework. We need a better understanding of Dave Snowden's work. In Agile development we are dealing with complex adaptive systems. That means we can't know in advance the effect of even a small change to our organizations, our teams, or ourselves. We can only test and then stop to reflect and based on our observation make plans for the next small change. It's delusional to believe that we can plan every activity over a long timeline of years for any effort.

I think you'll enjoy this easy-to-read, informative little book. I know I did.

—Linda Rising
Coauthor, with Mary Lynn Manns, of
Fearless Change and *More Fearless Change*

PREFACE

I'm Zuzi, your new friend and men-
tor. Relax and listen to what I'm going
to tell you. You can trust me. Ten years
ago, when I joined my first Scrum team
as a developer, I didn't like it much.
It was an awkward way of working, I
thought. I was just as resistant as most
of my current clients who are at the
beginning of their Agile journeys. It
was something new and different. And
however hard our Agile coaches tried to

explain it, I didn't really get it. Six months later I was appointed to
the ScrumMaster role. Lacking any other experience than as a team
leader and developer, I ended up being a "Scrum team assistant"
and a bit later a "Scrum team mom." It took me a long time to realize why Scrum is so powerful and that it is all about the ability to
enhance self-organization.

Only then did I realize that we were all missing a good expla-
nation of the ScrumMaster role. Later, I described it using the
#ScrumMasterWay concept that I'm going to share with you in this
book, and which finally gave ScrumMasters the answer to their
most common question: "What will the ScrumMaster do once the
team is self-organized?"

After coaching many ScrumMasters at companies and teaching a lot of CSM classes, I can say that an answer like "Move to another team," "Do nothing," or "There will always be some work needed" is not good enough. ScrumMasters are lost in the same way I was lost at that time.

It has never been so easy to become a great ScrumMaster, so let me invite you on the journey and you can learn from my experience and mistakes. This book is the best starting point to embrace the ScrumMaster role. I hope you will enjoy reading it and will find it useful and easy to apply in your work and that you will become a great ScrumMaster too.

WHO SHOULD READ THIS BOOK

This book is a guidebook for all ScrumMasters, Agile coaches, and leaders who want to transform their organizations. It's intended to give you a reference to general concepts every ScrumMaster should understand and point you toward resources that may help you in resolving difficult situations. It was designed as a slim, illustrated book that you can read during the weekend and won't get you lost in too much heavy stuff. However, it is supposed to be your starting point in searching for help or ideas on where to go next. On top of that, it's full of practical examples of how to apply each concept.

Note that the book does not explain Scrum rules and principles but assumes that you already understand Agile and Scrum and have some experience as a ScrumMaster.

HOW TO READ THIS BOOK

The book is divided into eight chapters which, step by step, create awareness and understanding of the great ScrumMaster's role.

In Chapter 1, "The ScrumMaster's Role and Responsibilities," we go through the basic responsibilities of the ScrumMaster.

In Chapter 2, "The State of Mind Model," I introduce the model that helps ScrumMasters decide which approach they will take to address day-to-day situations.

In Chapter 3, "#ScrumMasterWay," the #ScrumMasterWay concept is introduced to address the complexity of the role, the need to build a group of ScrumMasters, and through that create an Agile organization.

In Chapter 4, "Metaskills and Competences," we talk about what enables you to become a great ScrumMaster.

Chapter 5, "Building Teams," covers the theory of building teams, including practical examples relevant to the Agile environment.

Chapter 6, "Implementing Change," addresses the implementation and dynamics of change.

In Chapter 7, "The ScrumMaster's Toolbox," you will find a description of different tools you can use in your work as a ScrumMaster.

Chapter 8, "I Believe . . .," wraps things up.

The book provides a wider definition of the ScrumMaster's role than is usually described. It introduces the #ScrumMasterWay concept to define the three levels of operation of a great ScrumMaster. Being ScrumMaster is like playing in an adventure game. You pick up some tools along the way, and you don't necessarily understand how to use them at the beginning. Sometimes you need to be creative and try different approaches, taking some crazy steps. From time to time you might feel desperate and on the brink of quitting. But then you realize there is another way to approach the situation and make it work, like in those adventure games where you need to spot a tiny crack in the wall to open a secret door or apply the usual tools in a very different way.

Even if the examples might not fit your exact situation and the framework described might not feel appropriate during your first try, give it a second or third chance. Be creative and adapt these examples. Believe that it will work and, eventually, you will become a great ScrumMaster.

Register your copy of *The Great ScrumMaster* at informit.com for convenient access to downloads, updates, and corrections as they become available. To start the registration process, go to informit .com/register and log in or create an account. Enter the product ISBN (9780134657110) and click Submit. Once the process is complete, you will find any available bonus content under "Registered Products."

ACKNOWLEDGMENTS

Special thanks to my family for their support; without them I would not have been able to finish this book. Thanks to Arnošt Štěpánek for his honest feedback and the way he challenged me to rewrite some parts of the book. Thanks to ScrumMasters Hana Farkaš and Jiří Zámečník for their final review. Finally, I want to thank all the Scrum teams and ScrumMasters I coached during my Agile journey for their inspiration.

ABOUT THE AUTHOR

Zuzana Šochová, Agile Coach and Certified Scrum Trainer (CST), has over 15 years of experience in the IT industry. She led one of the very first Agile international projects in the Czech Republic, focusing on distributed Scrum teams, working in different time zones between Europe and the United States. Now she is a leading expert on Agile and Scrum practices in both start-ups and big corporations. She has experience with Agile adoption in telco, finance, health care, automotive, mobile, and high-tech software companies. She's been helping companies with Agile and Scrum across Europe, India, Southeast Asia, and the United States.

She has worked in various positions, starting as a software developer for life- and mission-critical systems, continuing as a ScrumMaster and director of engineering. She has been working as an independent Agile coach and trainer since 2010, specializing in organizational and team coaching, facilitations, and culture change using Agile and Scrum.

Zuzi is a well-known international speaker. She is a founder of the Czech Agile Community which organizes the annual Agile

Prague Conference. She is a Certified Scrum Trainer with Scrum Alliance. She received her MBA from Sheffield Hallam University (Great Britain) and her master's in computer science and computer graphics from the Czech Technical University. She coauthored the book *Agile Methods Project Management* (Computer Press, 2014), written in the Czech language.

twitter: @zuzuzka
web: sochova.com
blog: agile-scrum.com

Book page: greatscrummaster.com

1
. . .

THE SCRUMMASTER'S ROLE
AND RESPONSIBILITIES

The ScrumMaster is one of the most undervalued roles in Scrum and Agile. Most teams that are just starting out don't see the value of having a full-time ScrumMaster, and they try to combine this position with that of a developer or tester so that the ScrumMaster is "working." It's one of the most common misunderstandings of the ScrumMaster's role, and the majority of novice groups struggle with it. They say, "We understand that team members have to produce the software product; they are working hard. They have to learn cross-functionality and help each other. They have to cooperate. We also feel good about the Product Owner's role because that person has to define a vision and negotiate requirements with customers. But what about the ScrumMaster? What does he do?" Therefore, the ScrumMaster in such an environment often ends up as the secretary of the team—quite a boring position, right? Such a ScrumMaster takes care of the cards on the Scrum Board, removes every obstacle himself right away, and is close to making coffee for the team so they can focus solely on work. Sound familiar? Then continue reading, because this is definitely not even close to the intended role.

Another common misinterpretation of the role occurs in an environment where someone assumes the ScrumMaster role just because the company must implement Scrum—usually in a big corporation. People often say, "We have to have a ScrumMaster to do Scrum, right? But we can't use a good developer or QA because they have to do programming/testing." So the ScrumMaster in such an environment is often a wimpy, quiet person whose qualifications for being promoted to ScrumMaster are that he is not a good developer.

Bearing this in mind, the good ScrumMaster can't be seen as an additional expense—as someone who is not doing anything useful. He needs to be seen as the way to skyrocket the team's performance. A ScrumMaster aims to have not just a good team but a high-performing team. And in such a team, a ScrumMaster more than pays off.

Remember

- The ScrumMaster is not the secretary of the team.
- ScrumMasters aren't just an additional expense; they create high-performing teams.
- The ScrumMaster is an expert on the Agile and Scrum mindset and a true believer that Agile and Scrum are the right ways to be successful.

THE SELF-ORGANIZED TEAM

One of the key phrases of Scrum is the **self-organized team**. Everybody talks about it, but it's difficult to understand it and hard to develop it.

The self-organized team is an entity that can decide how to handle day-to-day tasks. In Scrum, it's limited to "How should we organize ourselves so we can deliver the Sprint Goal and Sprint Backlog to an agreed-upon quality specified by the Definition of Done?" In other words, the team should be able to decide who is

going to work on which task, how team members can help each other, when they need to learn something new, and how they prioritize their daily work in the absence of external authority.

Some teams believe that self-organization grants them unlimited power to decide anything on the planet. That isn't what is meant by the self-organized team in Scrum. Every self-organized team is self-organized only inside the given boundaries. Scrum boundaries are determined by the process—limited by Sprint Goals, Backlog, and delivering working product at the end.

If some team members are not happy with something, everyone on the team has to discuss it, understand each other, and, as a result, change their ways of collaborating and helping each other. The most important characteristic is the mindset of every individual. The good team has an attitude of "we" instead of "I": "How can I *help the team to solve it*? What can I do *for the others*?" instead of "*I don't know* anything about it. This is *not my problem*."

The self-organized team is a living organism, and every team member affects how strong or weak this organism will be. Team members who take responsibility and start to be accountable for the self-organized team entity instead of themselves as individuals are one step closer to being part of a great team.

The ScrumMaster's role is to support team rather than individual behavior. He must create such a team from individuals by reminding them that the team is an entity and is more important than individuals. He must always encourage team members to help others, rather than hide behind their own tasks.

A Group of Individuals

Jon is frustrated. It happens again and again, always the same old problem. So he finally approaches the team and says, "I didn't get any data from the system again! Have you got any ideas for how to fix it?"

See the reactions from the team:

> Fred: "Well, that's bad."
> Jean [*thinks*]: I'm glad I didn't choose that task today.
> Ron: "It was fine when I tried it yesterday."
> Jane: "It helped me to restart my PC last night."

Summary: It's bad all around, and Jon is on his own trying to solve the problem. It's his task; the others have enough on their plates. They might shout some advice, but no one looks at the problem from a higher perspective and takes responsibility for solving it.

The Real Team

Jon is frustrated. It happens again and again, always the same old problem. So he finally approaches the team and says, "I didn't get any data from the system again! Have you got any ideas for how to fix it?"

THE SELF-ORGANIZED TEAM • • • 5

See the reactions from the team:

> Jean: "I can have a look at Git to see if anybody made any changes."
>
> Jane: "I can try from my PC to check if I have the same problem, and then we can investigate together."
>
> Ron: "It's starting to bother us too often. . . . I'll think about some automation test to identify the problem earlier."
>
> Fred: "You're right; I'll help you with the test."

Summary: Team members come to the discussion with offers to solve the problem. They not only give advice, but they are also ready to put some effort into helping to solve it. They look at it from a team perspective and come up with ideas that will help the team.

Exercise: The Self-Organized Team

Complete the following statements (select the option you like the most) from the team member perspective and assess your team:

The most important thing for team members is to
   a. have their tasks ready by the promised time because others rely on them.
   b. offer help only if they feel they have time for it.
   c. help the team with whatever needs to be done.

The efficiency of each individual team member
   a. is key; each person has to be as efficient as possible.
   b. is important, but sometimes we need to help with something we don't know about and learn.
   c. is unimportant; the only thing that matters is the overall value delivered by the whole team.

If our team encounters an obstacle outside the team,
- a. we call our manager/team leader to tell us what to do or to solve it.
- b. we call the ScrumMaster to fix it for us.
- c. we have a team discussion about how we can overcome it and make it work for us.

When there is a task that seems to be too hard,
- a. we stay quiet and wait for someone else to take it on.
- b. we pass it to the most experienced team member because it is clearly his responsibility.
- c. someone expresses fear and initiates a discussion about how to approach the task as a team.

A team member is complaining about some tiny issue;
- a. it's clearly a tiny detail we don't care about.
- b. let the team vote on what to do.
- c. be curious and ask why he is frustrated about such a minor thing.

My colleague is insisting on something I don't agree with, so
- a. I do it my way; my colleague can do it his way.
- b. I ask the senior architect to support my way.
- c. I try to understand my colleague's solution and discuss the pros and cons of both approaches with the team before we all agree.

Give yourself no points for each "a" answer, 1 point for each "b" answer, and 2 points for each "c" answer, and then total your points. A score of 7 or above means your team has real self-organization.

THE SCRUMMASTER'S GOAL

The ScrumMaster has many responsibilities. Because it is hard to link them to any role in the traditional world, it's hard to understand what he is really doing all day. Great ScrumMasters must be practiced in soft skills and be good listeners. They must also be experts in Agile and Scrum. Preferably, they need to have experience on a Scrum team or in a Scrum environment. Otherwise, it will be difficult for them to enforce the Agile mindset and self-organization as general principles at every level.

So, what is the goal of the ScrumMaster? The ScrumMaster seeks to build a self-organized team and enforce self-organization as a key company principle at every level. Self-organization brings ownership and responsibility; it makes people more active and accountable. It gives them an opportunity to come up with their own solutions and makes the whole group more efficient. Self-organization is the key aspect of high-performing teams, not in the short term but in the long term. It provides an opportunity to improve and adapt processes, communication, and collaboration as needed. It generates highly motivated individuals, and as it is applied to a group of people, it helps to build them into a team—a team with one goal and a joint identity.

If instead ScrumMasters focus on any other responsibility as a goal, they end up becoming secretaries, advisers, managers, or just useless people who have "nothing to do, so we can ignore that role."

Remember

- The ScrumMaster's goal is to encourage self-organization.
- The ScrumMaster is a coach and facilitator.
- The ScrumMaster is not responsible for delivery.
- The ScrumMaster is not the team's secretary but should help the team remove impediments themselves.
- The ScrumMaster must encourage the team to take responsibility.

THE SCRUMMASTER'S RESPONSIBILITIES

The ScrumMaster's responsibilities include the following:

- Encourages the team to take responsibility and supports the team's single identity and goals
- Enables transparency and collaboration
- Removes impediments by encouraging the team to take over the activity
- Understands the Agile and Scrum mindsets and continuously educates himself
- Maintains Agile and Scrum values; helps others to understand and follow Scrum
- Protects the development team when needed
- Facilitates Scrum meetings
- Helps the team to become more efficient

PITFALLS OF COMBINING ROLES

If ScrumMasters combine multiple roles, they have to be good at distinguishing one from the other. They can wear only one hat at a time, so they have to choose which role they are in when speaking or acting. Otherwise, they won't be transparent, and both roles will suffer. The following examples provide more detail on the advantages and disadvantages of the roles most often combined with the ScrumMaster role.

The ScrumMaster Is a Team Member

Disadvantages. The ScrumMaster is too much engaged as a team member, so that he lacks system view and system thinking ability. He often lacks leadership and change management skills. Because he is a member of the team, he is usually less willing to improve the team, especially when the team has problems finishing a Sprint on time. He often lacks the ability to move the team to the next level.

Advantages. The ScrumMaster is part of the team; there is mutual trust between him and the team members. The ScrumMaster usually has a good understanding of Scrum basics and team weaknesses and can easily point them out at a Retrospective, that is, when tests are committed after the User Story is closed.

Result. The ScrumMaster role is usually treated as less important and often disappears altogether. The ScrumMaster is demoted to the level of a team assistant who has nothing to do anyway, so why not help the team with their work?

The ScrumMaster Is a Product Owner

Disadvantages. There is a huge conflict of interest because the ScrumMaster and Product Owner roles have conflicting goals. The ScrumMaster should never be responsible for delivery; that is the Product Owner's main goal. It's a conflict between business needs and team self-awareness. It's about balancing long-term versus short-term improvements and results.

Advantages. A Product Owner who is also a ScrumMaster is more likely to be treated as part of the team.

Result. In most cases the role of ScrumMaster is neglected and the Product Owner controls everything. Such a team usually lacks any deep Scrum understanding and self-organization.

The ScrumMaster Is a People Manager

Disadvantages: Such a ScrumMaster is often directive, relying on mentoring instead of coaching. His relationship with the team often lacks trust.

Advantages: Good managers are leaders and have experience with change management, so they catch on more quickly in the transformation period.

Result: The role of the ScrumMaster is usually treated as less important, but in certain cultures (not directive and less process oriented) this is a great opportunity to start Agile transformation. However, the dream job of most managers is not to become a ScrumMaster but to lead the organization, so they can fulfill the ScrumMaster role only temporarily. Despite the possible positive aspects, teams where the ScrumMaster is a manager often lack self-organization, self-confidence, and ownership because the manager, not the team, decides, fixes, and arranges.

The ScrumMaster Works with Multiple Teams

Disadvantages: A ScrumMaster for multiple teams lacks time, because even independent problems quite often arise at the same time. The inability to facilitate discussions early enough and prevent conflicts from growing often makes the job quite difficult.

Advantages: The ScrumMaster learns fast and is much more experienced in solving difficult problems. A general recommendation is to have one ScrumMaster for two teams, or a maximum of three teams, at one time. In most environments three would be way too many because such a ScrumMaster would lack the necessary information to prevent conflicts and move the teams to the next level.

Result: Such a ScrumMaster has more experience and is usually much better at system thinking because he understands that every team is different. Based on his experience of different environments, he is more likely to be successful in implementing Scrum in different cultures. He is also more likely to apply Scrum over the entire organization and will not be too attached to the development team.

Remember

- A ScrumMaster for two to three teams is the only recommended combination.
- The Product Owner should never act in the ScrumMaster role. The two roles have conflicting goals.
- The combination of ScrumMaster and manager often creates a lack of trust and makes the team too reliant on the manager's decisions, instead of taking responsibility themselves.

- The ScrumMaster should not be a team member. The ScrumMaster will miss the bigger picture and in most cases will prefer team member duties over ScrumMaster ones.
- The ScrumMaster should stay focused on one role at a time and not mix them. This is the only way to become a great ScrumMaster.

The ScrumMaster as a Servant Leader

Most ScrumMasters have trouble with the question "What does a ScrumMaster do during a Sprint?"

Empathy
Healing of relationships
Conceptualization
Stewardship
Commitment to the growth of others
Listening
Self-awareness
Persuasion
Foresight
Building community

That's what I will explain in the following chapters. But to give you the bottom line here, ScrumMaster is a leadership role. One of the aims of the ScrumMaster is to make others work better, by focusing not only on one Scrum team but on the overall organization. Are you surprised that the ScrumMaster must be a leader? So here it is. The ScrumMaster is not just someone who understands Scrum; he is much more than that. The ScrumMaster cares more about long-term goals and strategy than the short-term hard metrics. Leaders are not driven by time sheets. They have a vision, and they are self-driven and creative. You can call the ScrumMaster a servant leader, which actually refers to ancient Chinese philosophy. It's about "putting your team first, and yourself second" [1], and about improving yourself in the following areas:

- Listening to others
- Empathy
- Healing of relationships
- Awareness and self-awareness as a leader
- Use of persuasion rather than relying on positional authority
- Conceptualization—the ability to keep the bigger picture in mind and think beyond day-to-day realities and short-term goals
- Foresight—intuition that enables you to link lessons from the past with the current state and future decisions
- Stewardship—being open and serving others
- Commitment to the growth of others
- Building a community as a viable life form [2]

Remember

- ScrumMaster is a leadership position. It requires creativity, vision, and intuition to succeed.
- Good ScrumMasters are empathetic, good listeners, and ready to heal relationships.
- Great ScrumMasters are not solely focused on their teams but are able to build communities across the organization.

Exercise: Are You a Servant Leader?

Rate yourself as a ScrumMaster according to the characteristics of a servant leader on a scale of 1 to 10, where 1 means "I don't have it at all" and 10 means "That's my biggest strength."

_____

_____

_____

- Listening to others
- Empathy
- Healing relationships
- Awareness and self-awareness
- Persuasion
- Conceptualization
- Foresight
- Stewardship
- Commitment to the growth of others
- Building a community

Where would you like to improve the most and why?

Stay One Step Ahead

Any change is difficult, and every individual copes with it differently. Just as you can observe resistance in individuals, you can see it at the team or organization level. One of the ScrumMaster's roles is to be a guide during change such as an Agile transformation, a new way of collaborating, or a new practice. To be a good guide, the ScrumMaster must stay only one step ahead of the team and organization, pulling them out of their habits, norms, and customs. If he goes too far too fast, the team will most likely not understand what he is talking about. If, on the other hand, the ScrumMaster is at the same stage as they are, he is not challenging their status quo enough and they will not improve.

In the very first stage of the change, the ScrumMaster must overcome quite a bit of resistance—people will simply say, "We're happy with what we have." They don't want to change and don't see any need to change. So, asking them to take over some ownership and activity at this stage is bound to fail.

After some time people start saying, "It's all great, but it's not for us." They have already tried new things, but because it's not easy for them to change, they prefer to return to the previous state, before the change.

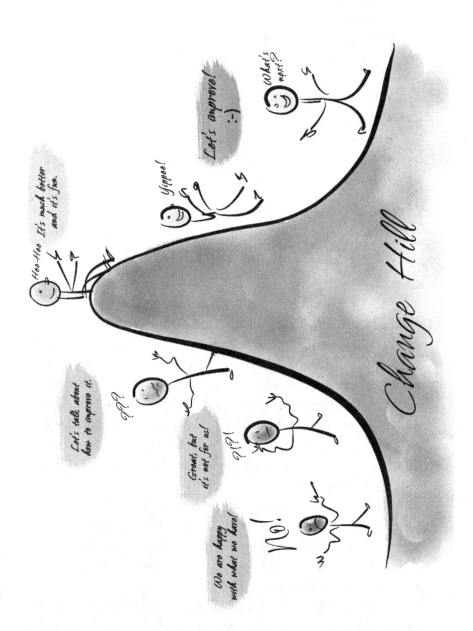

Sometime afterward, when together you have overcome the biggest issues, people will say, "Let's talk about how to improve things because we don't want to go back anymore." This is already a good state to be in.

Finally, they make it. And they celebrate. "It's much better than what we did before." And here is the biggest trap. They are all so happy with their achievement that they stop improving and get stuck. The ScrumMaster's role is to let them enjoy this moment but then to push them in the direction of more experimenting, process adaptation, and improvement.

Remember

- The ScrumMaster is a guide in Agile transformation.
- The ScrumMaster should stay only one step ahead of the team and organization, pulling them out of their habits and customs.

Hints for Great ScrumMasters

- Focus on self-organization; it's your ultimate goal.
- Don't mix different roles; be a full-time ScrumMaster.
- Believe in people; trust them to make it by themselves.
- Be a good guide during Agile transformation; stay only one step ahead at a time.
- Believe in Agile and Scrum. The great ScrumMaster is the biggest Agile enthusiast.
- The great ScrumMaster is a servant leader. Build a community, heal relationships, and listen to others.

2

. . .

THE STATE OF MIND MODEL

The ScrumMaster should adjust her approach according to the state of the team and the status of the company's Agile adoption. There is a useful model that can help the ScrumMaster decide which approach to take. It's called the ScrumMaster State of Mind [3], and it includes four core approaches:

- Teaching and mentoring
- Removing impediments
- Facilitation
- Coaching

I will describe them individually in the following pages.

Based on the maturity of the team and the fact that every team has different needs, the ScrumMaster will apply some approaches more frequently than others. Although all of them are useful at every team development stage, ScrumMasters should focus on the approach that helps them reach their current aim and supports the ultimate goal of enhancing self-organization.

After I describe the model, I'll give you a few examples, from real situations, of how the ScrumMaster State of Mind model can be useful.

TEACHING AND MENTORING

The teaching and mentoring approach is about sharing experiences of Scrum and Agile in general and using one's own experience to suggest additional practices and methods. At the beginning of Agile transformation, ScrumMasters have to explain the Agile and Scrum approach over and over again, because mentioning it once may not be enough for teams to understand why it is being implemented and how it should work. When the team has matured, it's more about experiences and suggestions for new practices than teaching, but it's still an important part of the ScrumMaster's job.

Teaching, Mentoring, and Sharing experiences

REMOVING IMPEDIMENTS

A great ScrumMaster should start each day with a question: "What can I do to make it easier for my team to perform their work?" One way of helping them is to remove impediments so they can work efficiently.

However, ScrumMaster is not just any administrative position, and so the way to remove impediments is to delegate responsibility, activities, and ownership to the team so they can solve problems by themselves. Unless the ScrumMaster gives the team the opportunity to take over these tasks, she ends up as their "smother" who is so loving and caring that her "kids" are low-confidence grown-ups, dependent on her even in their thirties.

So, should the ScrumMaster remove impediments? Yes, but in a way that supports the team in finding a solution. The ScrumMaster can start by explaining what self-organization is and why it is such an important part of Scrum and continue with coaching and facilitation.

Remove Impediments

FACILITATION

Facilitation means making sure that team meetings run smoothly and that communication flows in an efficient way. Therefore, every meeting or conversation should have a clearly defined goal, deliverables, and an idea of what the expected result looks like. The facilitation rule says you should never interfere with the content of the discussion or the solution itself. You only drive the discussion flow.

Remember

- Facilitation makes communication more efficient.
- Define a goal, deliverables, and expected results.

COACHING

Coaching is probably one of the most important skills the great ScrumMaster must have. It requires a lot of practice and experience, but once you master it, it's incredibly powerful. In Scrum, coaching focuses not only on an individual's personal growth, but also on team self-organization, responsibility, and ownership.

Remember

- Coaching is more powerful than explaining, sharing experiences, or giving advice.
- The goal is not to be fast in the short term but to improve in the long term.

EXAMPLE: STARTING AGILE

The team is at the beginning of the transformation. They've just passed Scrum training, but they still don't understand what it is really about. They complain that Scrum is not the right method for them.

The right approach here is to explain all over again (and repeatedly) why you do Scrum, what you expect from such change, and how individual Scrum meetings and artifacts work together. In order to be successful, team members have to understand the dynamics and principles behind Scrum. If the ScrumMaster only facilitates, most likely this will not happen fast enough. If the ScrumMaster coaches, the team will be lost, as they haven't a clue how to improve their Standup, for example.

EXAMPLE: IMPEDIMENTS

The team is taking over responsibility, but they face loads of problems.

The easiest way is to take over and remove those impediments for them. But wait. How does that approach lead to the goal of the ScrumMaster building a self-organized team? It doesn't. So the ScrumMaster has to take the slower and more painful approach for the sake of the team and coach them to realize they can handle most of the impediments by themselves. If the ScrumMaster doesn't do this, she ends up as team secretary very quickly, and the team becomes a low-confidence group that always waits for someone else to fix things. Proper facilitation of meetings and discussion helps as well.

EXAMPLE: STUCK

The team has been working in a Scrum environment for a long time. They may not be a good "Scrum team," but they are fine with how they are.

The optimal approach here would be coaching. Coaching techniques reveal opportunities for improvement to the team and also let the team members see their problems first. If the ScrumMaster starts with teaching and explaining, the team will most likely not accept it and reply that, as a self-organized team, they will decide how they work. The ScrumMaster is not there to tell them what to do. In some cases they refuse to accept such a ScrumMaster, and she has to leave eventually.

EXAMPLE: RESPONSIBILITY

The team is quite good; they mostly self-organize. The ScrumMaster remembers that her facilitation skills were a necessary aspect of their success. That's how the ScrumMaster improved their cooperation. That's how she made them efficient.

Nonetheless, it's the right time to move on and change the approach. All ScrumMasters should do is step back and let the team run the meeting. Don't stay in the middle, don't start it, and don't indicate who's next. Just be there, ready for facilitation with a lighter touch. Give them space and trust them. They will make it. If the discussion goes in the wrong direction, coach them so they identify the problem and adjust accordingly. Note that you are not disappearing at this time; you are still present, carefully listening, aware of what's going on, and ready to help if needed.

EXERCISE: STATE OF MIND—NOW

Go through all the approaches of the ScrumMaster State of Mind model and think about situations where taking this approach could be useful and also where it would be inappropriate.

Teaching, mentoring:

Removing impediments:

Facilitation:

Coaching:

Which approach is the most comfortable for you as a ScrumMaster and why?

- ☐ Teaching, mentoring, sharing experience, giving advice
- ☐ Removing impediments
- ☐ Facilitation
- ☐ Coaching

THE MISSING PIECE OF THE PUZZLE

Although all the approaches of the ScrumMaster State of Mind model are important during your journey to becoming a great ScrumMaster, one very important item is still missing—*observation*. If you take the opportunity to be quiet and let the team take over an activity, you can continue to observe them for another minute before you teach them or explain how they should do something, facilitate their conversation, coach them to decide themselves, or try to fix the problem yourself by removing impediments. If you resist the urge to solve every issue as quickly as possible so the team can get back to work again, you will be much closer to the goal of having a self-organized team.

Therefore, the ScrumMaster State of Mind model is very important, because it forces you to step back to the role of observer and decide which approach you are going to take and why. There is truth to the adage that listening is one of the most important aspects of communication and decision making.

When you imagine how listening could have improved the outcome while you were teaching, facilitating, coaching, and removing impediments, you will find some situations where you would have decided things differently if you had practiced this model.

Remember

- Observing, listening, and not interfering are the most important aspects of a great ScrumMaster's job.
- Any action, such as coaching, facilitation, teaching, or removing impediments, can wait until it's clear which approach is the best choice.

EXERCISE: STATE OF MIND—THE FUTURE

Is there any approach you would like to use more often? Why?

- ☐ Teaching, mentoring, sharing experiences, giving advice
- ☐ Removing impediments
- ☐ Facilitation
- ☐ Coaching
- ☐ Observation

Why?

_____

_____

_____

3

• • •

#SCRUMMASTERWAY

Scrum defines three roles only—ScrumMaster, Product Owner, and development team. The usefulness of the latter two is usually easy to understand, because companies can link them to existing roles, but the ScrumMaster role puzzles them.

To make the ScrumMaster role more understandable, I have designed a new concept describing three levels of a great ScrumMaster: #ScrumMasterWay. It helps ScrumMasters to focus

on the right level of the organization at any given time and pull them out of the development team perspective into that of the product and the overall organization.

Every level is individually described in the following sections, but before you go on, try this simple exercise.

EXERCISE: #SCRUMMASTERWAY

Complete the following statements from the ScrumMaster's point of view (select the option you like the most):

It is most important to me
    a. to have an efficient, happy development team that follows Scrum.
    b. to have a good relationship among members of the product group: Product Owner, development team(s), manager, and other stakeholders.
    c. to help the whole organization embrace the Agile mindset.

The Product Owner should be
    a. not part of any team; he should not attend Retrospectives.
    b. my partner; I'm here to help.
    c. a member of the self-organized team of Product Owners taking care of the product portfolio.

Other teams that need our input or support
    a. are spoken of as "them" and we don't care about their needs.
    b. have to ask the Product Owner to plan items into the Backlog.
    c. are part of our company and we help each other.

I expect the manager
    a. not to attend any team meetings.

    b. to help me create a suitable environment and remove some roadblocks.

    c. to support my learning and encourage me to come up with innovations and changes at the organizational level.

I expect to get

    a. clear and measurable expectations of what I am supposed to achieve.

    b. an opportunity to aim for long-term team success.

    c. the freedom to come up with innovative and creative ideas, even outside our group.

A group of ScrumMasters is

    a. useless, because I don't need other ScrumMasters to do my job.

    b. useful, because we can help each other and share experiences.

    c. the most important group because I can't "change the world"/my organization alone.

If you chose "a," you're at Level 1; "b," Level 2; "c," Level 3 (the levels will be explained in the following sections).

LEVEL 1—MY TEAM

At this level the ScrumMaster feels responsible for the development team only. It's not uncommon; it happens to most new ScrumMasters who have passed some training course and started to apply Scrum theory. During the class they are already struggling with questions such as "How can I make myself useful every day?"

    The answer goes back to the goal of the ScrumMaster: to build a self-organized development team, and let them embrace Scrum values and the Agile mindset, which is a long-term activity, not a

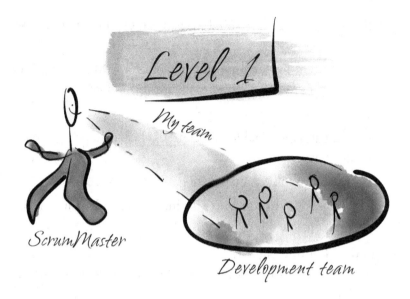

short-term task. Bearing this in mind, your first step would be to make yourself comfortable in the Observation segment from the ScrumMaster State of Mind model and suppress the urge to do something like removing impediments yourself or giving advice.

In this first transformation stage you would find yourself busy with the development team's resistance, lack of understanding, and absence of ownership, responsibility, and experience. When you have passed this phase, another question arises: "What shall I do when my team is finally self-organized?"

This makes perfect sense, because at the beginning Scrum-Masters must spend more time teaching and explaining and maybe also removing impediments, but at a certain point in time such activities may not be necessary anymore. Facilitation of team discussions and meetings may not be as necessary either. For example, a Standup meeting is simple enough that the team can run it independently without any ScrumMaster activity. At this time the ScrumMaster is ready for the next levels of the #ScrumMasterWay model, where there is plenty of work to be done.

Remember

- The first level of the #ScrumMasterWay model is good for the initial transformation phase, but it's just the start of your great ScrumMaster journey.

LEVEL 2—RELATIONSHIPS

You feel good about your team, but it's time to move to the second level and focus on relationships. The first step is to create a coherent, self-confident Scrum team that integrates the Product Owner into the team, and to create balanced relationships among the three Scrum roles.

When you are finished with that, your next step is to emphasize all the relationships and connections the Scrum team has—with customers, users, product people, marketing, support groups, and other teams and line managers. In this effort you are applying self-organization to everyone who is involved and building self-organized teams with the people who work with you. This can include the implementation of a scaling Scrum model (which will be described later in this book) or just focusing on the overall communication and information flow.

Consequently, the ScrumMaster's ability to explain Scrum at the development team level is a good background skill for this level. The crucial factor is your understanding and definition of Scrum as not only a set of meetings, roles, and artifacts but also a culture, philosophy, and mindset. In this stage you must see Scrum as an empirical process that you can imagine as a playground with certain boundaries around it and a few general rules for how to play, but the details of how to play are up to the team and will differ from one team to another.

In this stage, more flexible virtual teams are built to take over ownership and responsibility for certain areas. Some of these teams solve problems or address issues and then fade; some will remain active for a longer time. In this stage you are making continuous improvement and perpetual adaptation of your cooperation an integral part of your environment.

Remember

- The development team and Scrum team are not the only teams in an Agile organization.
- Scrum is a mindset, culture, and philosophy, not just a fixed set of practices.

LEVEL 3—ENTIRE SYSTEM

Finally, the last level of the #ScrumMasterWay model focuses on the organization or one of its parts as a whole system. At this level you want to transform the world of work by guiding the organization to become prosperous and sustainable, to inspire people, and to create value for society. That's actually the mission of the Scrum Alliance.

Level 3 moves the ScrumMaster's focus to the entire system, bringing the Agile mindset and Scrum values to the company level. It helps an organization to change its approach to its employees, management and leadership style, product ownership, and strategy, so it can be more flexible and welcoming of change.

The new understanding and definition of Scrum is "a way of living." It becomes a culture or philosophy according to which you can live. You realize that it's not only a way of working, but that you can apply these principles to your personal life. That doesn't mean doing family Standups, having a family Backlog, or anything like that. It's more about attitude, principles, and approaches.

The ScrumMaster at this level becomes an Agile or enterprise coach who is helping the organization to become more efficient, contented, and successful. Regardless of the situation, the ScrumMaster should be aware of the current status at all three levels, but his activity may vary depending on the circumstances. Note that unless the previous level is working well, you can't really jump to the next level.

Remember

- The ScrumMaster works as an Agile and enterprise coach, improving the whole organization.
- Scrum and Agile are a way of life.
- First fix the development team level, and then improve relationships before you focus on the system level.
- Make sure you still keep an eye on the lower levels so they improve as time goes by, aligned with the top levels.

Hints for Great ScrumMasters

- Observe before you decide which ScrumMaster State of Mind approach you are going to take.
- Remove impediments by helping the team to remove them.
- Facilitation is more than running a meeting, reading a book, or going to a facilitation class.
- Coaching is not about your experience but rather the ability to ask good questions.
- Work at all three levels of the #ScrumMasterWay model; don't stay only at your development team's level.
- Agile and Scrum are the ways the great ScrumMasters work and live.

THE SCRUMMASTERS' GROUP

If you want to move an organization to the next level, to be based on self-organization, high motivation, activity, and ownership from the bottom up, one of the core requirements is a strong group of ScrumMasters. If your organization's agility is supported by ScrumMasters operating at the #ScrumMasterWay "My Team" level, you are only creating and perfecting, which is a good starting point, but not a significant growth strategy to achieve your goal of *changing the way of working*. You may admit that you can create an Agile coach position, but even the greatest Agile coach can't change the organization alone. You need a self-organized team to be successful. So the best place to start is by creating a team of ScrumMasters.

The purpose of a ScrumMaster team is to help other people to be ready for the system level and then focus together on the whole system. The question is how to involve different people, how to build virtual and often temporary self-organized teams across the company structure, and how to enable people to get involved and take ownership.

THE ORGANIZATION AS A SYSTEM

Traditional methods for achieving the "next Agile state" fail because they are not based on self-organization and don't see the organization as a system but as a hierarchy. ScrumMasters who simply begin to operate at the Agile coach level usually struggle with the concept of the organization as a system. The reason for this is usually in their own heads. They approach the situation with methods that were useful on the previous two levels of the #ScrumMasterWay model, such as organizing workshops, explaining, bringing in new concepts, and coaching at the team level, yet they fail to see the organization as a system.

You would need to apply coaching at the system/enterprise level, and none of your goals would be short-term or in any way straightforward. What you need to do is based on Organization and Relationship Systems Coaching (ORSC) [4]. You would have to experiment, be playful and curious, and try different things to stimulate reactions. The system will give you some feedback, and all you

have to do is to believe that every system is naturally creative and intelligent, so the people in that system don't need you to tell them what to do. They will find out. However, they might not see it in the first instance, so they need you as a coach to challenge their status quo and reveal to them what you have seen from your different viewpoint.

Building a ScrumMaster team seems to be simple, but the reality is often hard. The following sections describe typical scenarios for such a process.

Remember

- To change the way of working, you have to adapt your style and approach.
- The first step in moving a company to the next level and creating an Agile organization is to build a strong team of ScrumMasters.
- Every organization is a system that is naturally creative and intelligent; the people in the system will figure out what to do.

First Attempt

It seems to be easy. "We have ScrumMasters, so let them meet regularly and let's make them into a team." They are teaching self-organization and applying it in their teams, so it should be a piece of cake to apply self-organization to a group of ScrumMasters. But once you introduce such an idea, you surprisingly get huge resistance:

"What for? I don't see any value in such a group."

"I don't need other ScrumMasters to help me with my team. They are different and their teams have different issues, so we will have different strategies."

"It's good to get advice from others when I'm struggling, but in such cases I can just go and ask directly."

Clearly the issue here is that ScrumMasters are working mostly at the #ScrumMasterWay "My Team" level, where such complaints make perfect sense.

Why should I care about other ScrumMasters?

ScrumMaster

It's me and my team

ScrumMaster

me, me, me

ScrumMaster

ScrumMasters' team
Why?

ScrumMaster

ScrumMaster's Land

The first step is explaining to the ScrumMasters their role in the context of the #ScrumMasterWay model. Then you can move on to building a ScrumMasters' team. At the beginning, only a small group of ScrumMasters might be ready to move on to the next level, which is perfectly fine.

Note that it's a huge step for most of them. You are asking them to leave their classical world where they got quite clear and measurable goals from their managers—for example, "Apply Scrum and make the team efficient"—into a world of uncertainty and creativity where they are asked to change the culture and apply a different type of leadership. The expectation here could be, for example, "Make the organization more active, involved, and self-confident."

First Steps

- Explain the #ScrumMasterWay model and let ScrumMasters self-evaluate where they are most of the time.

- Make sure they understand why they should move to the next level (the reply that "the #ScrumMasterWay model says so" is not enough).
- Create a core team that is advanced enough to understand the vision of the ScrumMasters' group.

The ScrumMaster's Land

So here it is—the ScrumMaster's Land. Let's assume that during the past months you've built a good, self-organized team of ScrumMasters who are trying to improve the environment and increase the level of agility. Are you finished? Not quite. ScrumMasters usually still have to focus on how others will change, so they are more aligned with how we work, not blocking us, not preventing us from doing Scrum and Agile as well. It's surprising that they tend to make the same mistake their team members used to make, saying, "The others should change" and "They have to understand." The way this group tries to achieve such a change is aligned with that perception—organize training that may be interesting for them, but the principles may be hard to apply in their day-to-day work.

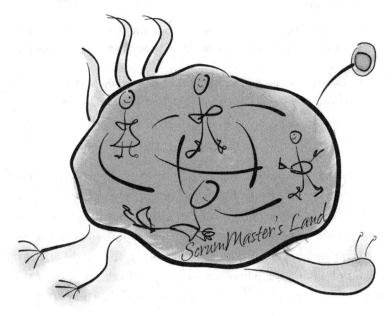

There are two constraints that prevent ScrumMasters from succeeding at this level—a lack of system thinking and system view, which is described in the next section, and a lack of change management experience. Also, it's all connected to the meaning of Scrum. At this stage they are still mostly oriented to the #ScrumMasterWay "Relationships" level. It's all about "us." When you ask why "they" (support, marketing, sales, managers, other teams) should be more Agile, the most common answer is because we need it: "We use Scrum now, and we can't create any fixed plans, so they should change and be more flexible." But it's the opposite approach that is needed. Start looking at it from their perspective. Use their point of view and answer the question "What is in it for them? Why should they change?" or "Why should the company be more Agile?" Once you understand their point of view, you can start a new Agile transformation. It's the same tough effort that it was to switch a few developers and testers to Scrum some time ago. It's a huge change. And you are here to make it work.

First Steps

- It's not about what we need from you. Look at it from their point of view; understand their needs, fears, and perspectives.
- To apply Agile and Scrum is not the goal; these are just useful tools to help you change culture and become *better*.

Change the World

The last stage is about the ability to understand the system point of view—see the whole thing. Don't get bogged down in the details. It's the same as in the team view. Once you start to see the team as a system, no particular process divergences are important anymore, nor are any individual people issues. It's like being at a height of 10,000 feet and observing the whole world below. Think about what matters from such a point of view. Scrum is an empirical process. There

ScrumMaster's Land

are certain boundaries and rules around the Scrum playground that should be followed at any time. However, most of the issues that bother you as a ScrumMaster can wait. They are unimportant from the point of view of the system. And if some issues still bother you, coach the entire team so it can realize that as well. Make the situation even more painful so it will help the team to come up with the first step toward adjusting their behavior.

This is the same approach that ScrumMasters need to apply at the level of the whole organization. It's just that the system is bigger and more complex. It's harder to coach, harder to see as a whole, harder to understand. The concept used here is called Systems Thinking [5].

The important things to focus on at the system level are the relationships and dynamics among them. Before every change, it's great to start drawing parts and entities on a flipchart and then identify how they influence each other. Think about the positive impacts but also the negative ones. Search for loops that multiply both effects. It's definitely a group activity, so use it as a tool to start a discussion about how to go about changing the company.

Another great tool for approaching complex systems is the application of impact mapping [6] (described in the same-named section in Chapter 7, "The ScrumMaster's Toolbox") to your goal—changing the system. It was originally a product management tool: "Impact mapping can help you build products and deliver projects that make an impact, not just ship software" [7]. But it's perfectly applicable here as well, because it reinforces the system view and describes all actors, impacts, and deliverables.

First Steps

- The important things to focus on at the system level are the relationships and dynamics among them.
- Draw a system map of your organization to see what influences your system and how.

CYNEFIN FRAMEWORK

As a ScrumMaster you should be able to classify problems and situations and, based on those classifications, decide what approach to take. Cynefin is a useful framework, described by David Snowden

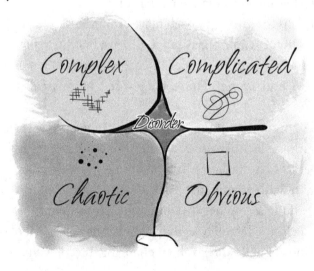

[8], which categorizes problems into five domains: obvious, complicated, complex, chaotic, and disorder. During your software product development you will bump into all of them. However, most software development work will be classified as complex.

Obvious

If all your problems were simple, the solutions would be obvious and there would be no issue about selecting the right approach. It would be the world of *best practices*. Just recognize the situation, categorize it, and apply a predefined solution.

Complicated

However, some situations are not so simple and require some analysis to classify them. In this domain we ask experts to suggest a solution. We believe that during the analysis we can answer the questions that need to be answered to make our final decision. Sound familiar? That's what classical waterfall does, right?

The complicated domain is the world of *good practices* that are well planned and chosen after a decent amount of analysis.

Complex

Unfortunately, some situations are neither simple nor complicated. Such cases are hard to assess up front, so even deep analyses fail, and the only way out is to allow *emergent practices* to appear. This is the world you are creating with Agile and Scrum.

Even if software development is said to be in a complex domain, certain situations you face are simple; for those you use prescription solutions, like continuous integration, Standup meetings, Sprints, Retrospectives, and Scrum boards. Some of them are complicated, for which you use good practices—for example, particular ways the Scrum Board is organized, the form of Backlog Items, product architecture, usability, and the application of root-cause analysis. Nonetheless, most situations cannot be solved with analyses or using your experiences, and in such complex situations you need to be more dynamic and inspect and adapt. That's exactly how Scrum works. Implement Kaizen and regularly run experiments each Sprint. Based on the knowledge gained about the complexity of your communications, cooperation, and the ways of working, you adapt.

Chaotic

The next domain is called chaotic. David Snowden often gives an example of a children's party. It's completely unpredictable, and every attempt to control it fails. It's the world of "novel practices." You need to come up with extraordinary and unusual solutions to get it under control.

Such situations happen in the work environment as well. For example, a critical bug stops your entire company and customers. You need to fix it right away. "Your initial solution may not be the best, but as long as it works, it's good enough. Once you've stopped the bleeding, you can take a breath and determine a real solution" [9].

Disorder

Finally, there is the disorder area. In this middle part of the Cynefin concept you don't know yet how to classify the situation, and so you mostly apply the approach you are used to. It's in your comfort zone, but it often fails.

The Cynefin domain boundaries are not strict, and sometimes it's hard to recognize which quadrant you are grounded in. The most dangerous area is the boundary between obvious and chaotic, where a wrong assessment may lead to an absolute disaster.

Exercise: Cynefin Framework

Look at the problems and situations you've faced in the last couple of Sprints and classify them according to the Cynefin framework:

- Obvious: _____
- Complicated: _____
- Complex: _____
- Chaotic: _____

4

. . .

METASKILLS AND COMPETENCES

By now you might be thinking about the great ScrumMaster profile. How does the great ScrumMaster think? What skills does she need to acquire in order to become a great ScrumMaster? In what areas does she need to be experienced in order to be successful? What competences do the great ScrumMasters need to gain?

METASKILLS

Metaskills are intentionally chosen attitudes to a situation, philosophy, or stance. They are cognitive strategies that an individual applies to new situations based on experience from previous ones. Instead of specialization, we talk about the generalization of that skill. Metaskills are abstract skills that allow some other more specific skills to emerge.

The ScrumMaster's Metaskills

Let's look at the most important metaskills every ScrumMaster has to have:

- Teaching
- Listening
- Curiosity
- Respect
- Playfulness
- Patience

It's very important to choose the appropriate one for each situation and intentionally use it. For example, if you join a discussion with the core metaskill of curiosity, you will act differently than you would if you had chosen listening or teaching.

Different situations call for different metaskills, and you don't need to stick with the one you selected at the beginning through the whole situation. But the change of metaskill should be done intentionally rather than just doing something you have gotten used to.

Remember

- For every situation, choose one core metaskill and use it during the event.
- Each metaskill is useful in a different situation.
- Always choose metaskills intentionally before you act.

Exercise: Metaskills

Think about situations where using each of these metaskills would be valuable:

- Teaching: _____
- Listening: _____
- Curiosity: _____
- Respect: _____
- Playfulness: _____
- Patience: _____

COMPETENCES

Let's look at the competences and areas of experience every Scrum-Master should have. The following sections describe the most important ones [10].

Master of Agile

First of all, ScrumMasters have to be masters of Agile. They should have experience with a Scrum team or an Agile environment; otherwise it will be quite a challenge for them to implement Scrum from scratch. The experience of a self-organized environment is crucial. Also, some experience of Agile development practices, testing, Agile leadership and management, Agile product ownership, and large-scale Scrum implementations would be very helpful. On top of that, some general understanding of Lean principles, Kanban, and Extreme Programming is useful as well.

But theory alone is not enough. ScrumMasters need to search for additional resources to get some insight. Attending conferences and discussing real situations with other participants and speakers is one option. Joining user group events is another. Most conferences record videos from their talks so you don't even have to travel. The Agile community is very active, so hundreds of new blog posts,

articles, and case studies are published every day, which makes following new trends in Agile and Scrum quite easy and accessible.

Mastering Agile includes the ability to generalize the simple Scrum principles and apply them to different environments from the ones they described originally. Do experiments and share the results with others. The "inspect and adapt" principle is about learning from failure. So make failure in the company an integral part of your learning process.

Explaining and Experience

This part of the competence map is linked to the teaching metaskill. Moreover, every great ScrumMaster must be able to sell these concepts to different audiences and make them keen and enthusiastic.

Without real-life experience it would be a challenge to adopt certain practices and artifacts or even implement core meetings in an efficient way.

But there is more—for example, you can share such experiences internally in your company, organize mutual visits in cooperation with another company, and so on.

Facilitation and Coaching

On the other side of the spectrum are facilitation and coaching where you suppress any experience you have, apply the metaskills of listening and curiosity, and let the team decide. As a facilitator, you are responsible for framing the discussion, not for the content. Facilitation is about not only making sure meetings happen but also how to make them efficient and valuable. If you do it right, teams stop complaining that "Scrum is only about meetings" because their discussions will have clear meaning and will flow in an efficient manner.

The most important realization in coaching is that it's not about your understanding, or your advice or suggestions. As a good coach you ask so-called powerful questions to let the team realize what they want and why. Note that unless you truly believe that people are able to come up with a better solution than you have in mind, coaching will be very difficult for you. To summarize, coaching is not about giving advice, but about supporting people to come up with their own solutions. If you ask the right questions, they always will.

CORE COMPETENCES

There are three core competences the ScrumMaster should have. She doesn't have to have deep knowledge of any of these—such expert notions may prevent the ScrumMaster from being a good facilitator and coach—but she should use them as a "spice." These three competences are so different that it's difficult to gain deep experience in every one of them. However, a little know-how concerning each is extremely helpful.

Business knowledge may not be so important at the "My Team" level of the #ScrumMasterWay concept, because the Product Owner role is responsible for such connections. But in the next two levels the ScrumMaster should be able to teach and advise Product Owners on Agile product ownership and introduce new practices and concepts for managing a product portfolio.

Change management is especially useful, because ScrumMasters are the ones who introduce change to the company. The change can be either a huge one, which the Japanese call Kaikaku, or a small one, which they call Kaizen.

Kaikaku is a radical breakthrough change that happens only from time to time. It's difficult, and it creates quite a lot of resistance, like moving from traditional management into Agile. On the other hand, there is the small evolutionary and incremental improvement called Kaizen. That's the purpose of Scrum Retrospectives. Just identify the first step that may immediately improve how you work now, for example, applying the rule "One User Story at a time."

Technical knowledge is also good, not because the ScrumMaster can advise the team on how to write code or even write the code for them, but because she can advise at the level of development practices. The focus here is on Extreme Programming practices like shared code, simplicity, continuous refactoring, pair programming, continuous integration, test automation, or test-driven development. The ScrumMaster's technical background can be extremely useful when introducing such technical practices.

Exercise: Which Competences Do You Have?

Study the following two examples and then use the empty chart to assess your current situation. First, identify reality—how well you currently practice the competences—by shading each wedge. Then use a different color of shading to indicate the areas you would like to improve. The middle of the circle is "not good: ☹"; the edges stand for "great: ☺."

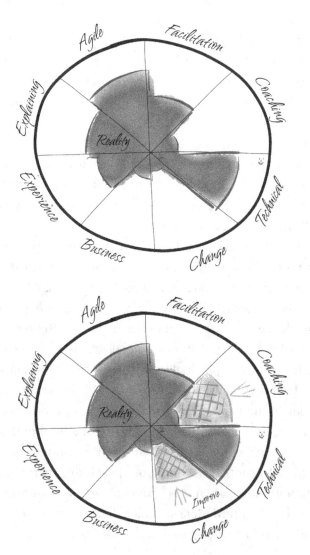

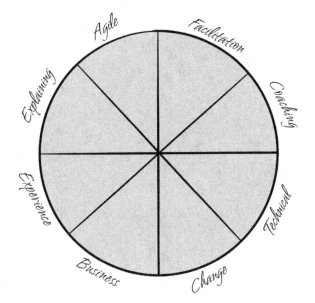

Hints for Great ScrumMasters

- Look at the organization as a system.
- Build a real team of ScrumMasters to address organizational complexity.
- Intentionally bring the metaskills of curiosity, playfulness, respect, and patience into everyday situations.
- The ScrumMaster is never finished with learning. Follow blogs, read books, watch videos, and select one specific class each year to improve a selected competence.

5

• • •

BUILDING TEAMS

The ability to build great teams is one of the most important competences the great ScrumMaster has to have. The following concepts
will give you a better idea of how to differentiate great teams from
teams that are just OK, how to improve dysfunctional teams, and how
to create an environment where teams can grow and become great.

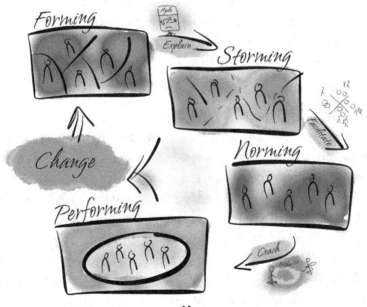

TUCKMAN'S GROUP DEVELOPMENT

One of the classical theories of team development is Tuckman's model of the stages of group development [11]. Let's look at how this theory applies to the Scrum environment. Imagine you've just started Agile transformation and are moving to Scrum. You've got a bunch of individuals that you call a team, specifically a self-organized Scrum team that is supposed to become cross-functional. So what's happening?

Forming

Being in the forming stage is kind of OK. People don't talk or cooperate much; they still keep their old habits as individual specialists. They actually don't need each other. Scrum is hard to apply to their way of working, so they complain that it's not at all useful in their environment.

The ScrumMaster's role at this stage is to explain the backbone Scrum principles and start the transformation, not only on paper but in the team's heads—to lift them out of their habits. ScrumMasters have to be present in all segments of the ScrumMaster State of Mind model; however, they spend significantly more time teaching, explaining, and sharing experiences.

Storming

Storming usually comes very soon after forming, because Scrum pushes cooperation, commitment, and communication far beyond the team's limits. The tension grows as they try to follow the Scrum process; they start to argue with each other and often get upset. It's not a happy place to be, so they are glad to grasp any hand being offered to them to get out of this stage.

The ScrumMaster's role is to encourage them to talk and make working agreements on how they are going to act together. In this stage the most important aspect of the ScrumMaster State of

Mind model would be facilitation, because smooth communication may take the team out of storming to the next stage of norming, whereas poor communication can break them apart and turn them into a dysfunctional team.

Norming

The norming stage brings liberation from stress and the team can finally breathe. "Wow, it finally works," they say. "And it's better than before! We like it." But be aware that this is exactly the reason why norming is so dangerous: it tempts teams to stay where they are: "We are good; we don't have to improve anymore." But that's not the goal. You didn't put in all that effort to end up here. A good team is not yet the high-performing one that you aimed for.

The role of the ScrumMaster is to show the team ways to get even better. Encourage them to take ownership and responsibility and continue improving. In the ScrumMaster State of Mind model, the most important tool to be used at this stage is coaching. Without it they are likely to get stuck in this stage forever—which is not too bad, because this stage is already quite comfortable and productive.

Performing

Nevertheless, the real goal you want to achieve with Scrum is the performing stage. This is the right Scrum team. So how do you recognize you are there? First of all, the team is self-confident and always looks for better ways to do things. They don't feel they are finished yet. They are playful, they run experiments, and they are not afraid of failing. They are open and transparent. They are not self-centered but looking across their team boundaries. It's a very creative and innovative place to work, and the people have lots of fun.

What is the ScrumMaster's role here? Well, to prevent things from going wrong and avoid the team returning to any previous stage. It is mostly observing, while focusing on other levels of the #ScrumMasterWay, always being ready to step in as coach, facilitator, or impediments remover or to share experiences and teach the team new things.

Change

To complete the model, there is always some change. And even a small change (such as when one person leaves or joins a team) can break a team apart and make them return to the first forming stage. They will most likely not stay there for a long time, but they may have to go through all the team development model stages again. It may take a day, or forever, because they might get stuck at the norming stage this time. If you think about it, it makes perfect sense: during the first round the ScrumMaster was diligently taking care of communication, working agreements, and team health, but this time it may be that no one thinks about these things.

Thus the ScrumMaster's role must be to observe any change and to identify it early and adjust his behavior regarding the actual team stage, even if it's just for a couple of days. For the same reason, even a great self-organized team needs the ScrumMaster. Otherwise, they may not handle such changes by themselves and eventually end up in the norming or storming phase.

Exercise: Using Tuckman's Group Development

At which level is your team right now?

- ☐ Forming
- ☐ Storming
- ☐ Norming
- ☐ Performing

Write down some action steps to take next.

_____

_____

_____

FIVE DYSFUNCTIONS OF A TEAM

Sometimes a group of people happens to be quite far from being a great team. One concept that addresses this situation is based on the book by Patrick Lencioni, *The Five Dysfunctions of a Team* [12]. The concept is represented as a pyramid with the more basic layers at the bottom, and every team must excel at each level. Nevertheless, before you can expect your team's commitment, they must trust each other and be able to communicate in an efficient and honest manner, even if they don't agree with each other. Let's look at how this model applies in the Agile environment.

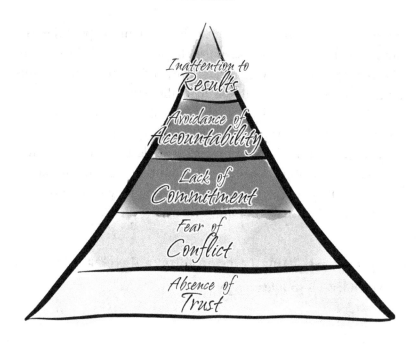

Absence of Trust

If asked, team members rarely admit to an absence of trust. They say they have known each other for a long time and they have no problems with each other, so what's the point of asking about trust? However, they are quiet, they work individually, and the fear of being vulnerable inhibits them from any further discussion and cooperation. Such team members don't need each other. At that level each single individual believes he has some specialization or specific technical knowledge or domain know-how that the others don't have. Team members protect their status quo and maintain the silos.

Fear of Conflict

If team members avoid conflicts, they tend to preserve an artificial harmony. Just as in the storming phase in the Tuckman model, team members try to avoid any discussion that could become difficult and so keep the work divided into individual, separate, disjunctive

areas based on technical or product knowledge and stick to the silos they currently have. You hear things like "Why should we spend time in discussion when we have separate areas to work on?" or "It doesn't make sense to cooperate on one User Story; it only leads to unnecessary confusion in communication."

Lack of Commitment

This team dysfunction is quite common at the beginning of the Agile journey. You can easily recognize it when people say, "We can't say what we will finish by the end of the Sprint—anything can happen" or "I will finish my part, but I can't speak for the others." Also, teams typically admit that they struggle with commitment, but their problems are usually rooted in the lower level of absence of trust.

Avoidance of Accountability

Most of us have seen a Scrum team that plans a Sprint but doesn't finish all the Sprint Backlog Items. At the end of the Sprint they call it an exception for some reason or another and plan the same amount of work for the next Sprint. It can happen to every team from time to time, but if it is a regular occurrence, it's clearly a dysfunction.

Inattention to Results

The final layer of the dysfunction pyramid is inattention to results or, in other words, having individual goals instead of one common goal.

And a common goal is exactly what we try to achieve with Scrum. Instead of each individual keeping his know-how and finishing his code and test, there should be a single team goal to deliver value to the customer. It's a huge mind shift, but it's crucial for success.

The ScrumMaster's Role

So what should the ScrumMaster do? First, identify how deep in the dysfunctions pyramid his team is. Once he recognizes this, he has to teach the team to increase their understanding, coach them to make them realize they have a problem, and help them to create some team alliance or working agreement on how they are going to work together. The key is the realization of what the team wants to achieve and why, plus some plan for how they are going to get there.

One small piece of advice that helps when you've risen beyond the initial layers is to create a team identity intentionally. Call them "the team," and let them decide on a name. Never ask individuals what they think—always make the team accountable. "What does the team think about it?" or "You are the team, you should decide." You'll be surprised at how well such a tiny change works.

Exercise: The Dysfunctional Team

Which dysfunctions can you recognize in your team?

- ☐ Inattention to results
- ☐ Avoidance of accountability
- ☐ Lack of commitment
- ☐ Fear of conflict
- ☐ Absence of trust

What are your next steps?

_____

_____

_____

TEAM TOXINS

Even a good team can sometimes fall short when it comes to supportiveness, collaboration, and friendly behavior. Let me introduce you to four toxins [13] that often poison teams and organizations. It's good to be aware of all four of them and, if they emerge, to identify them and help the team to overcome such situations.

Blame

Everyone does this sometimes: "It's your fault!" It's easy and natural to try not to be responsible for any faults.

In a Scrum team it can be a complaint like "It is the Product Owner's fault. He is responsible for the Backlog and User Stories. This one was just not well described," instead of saying, "This User Story was not defined well; what shall we do with it next time so it will never happen again?"

Defensiveness

Defensiveness is the second most common toxic behavior that the good team has to avoid. It often starts as a response to blaming. Continuing with the previous example, the Product Owner may reply, "It's not my fault! I'm not planning the Sprint Backlog. Moreover, it went through Grooming, plus this User Story had the same details as others."

Another situation could be a team that is defensive whenever anyone suggests any change. It starts with quite innocent advice:

Team: "In your experience, what are other teams doing on top of what you've seen here?" or "How do different companies apply Scrum?"

Coach: "Recently, there has been a strong trend toward one-week Sprints, so many companies are going in that direction now."

Team: "But we are doing two weeks for a reason. We can't move into one week. Our projects are too complex."

Coach: "You don't have to switch it next Sprint, but you may want to discuss what would have to change in order to go for the one-week Sprint and then decide."

Team: "No. We've just started and . . . by the way, we've had good results with two weeks already."

Stonewalling

The third team toxin is quite common as well. It's about repeating one's own idea over and over again and not listening to the arguments of other people.

The typical example from a Scrum team could be during the estimation meeting when the team is discussing arguments to get agreement and understanding and one team member says, "For me it's 5!" Quite common, isn't it?

Another situation might be the splitting of decisions and avoiding any discussion about them: "I'm working on it, so I do it my way; when you do it next time, you can choose your way." This one is not as straightforward as the first one, but after all it has the same result.

If you do things this way, you don't work as a team, but as a group of individuals who have little in common.

Contempt

A bit of irony is part of life. There is nothing wrong with it. The British sense of humor, for example, is famous worldwide. However, there is a thin line beyond which irony becomes sarcasm. It starts to be critical when team agreement is far away and you are searching for alignment. Then any comment like "Yep, you've never underestimated anything" can make things worse.

In general, every statement you make with the intention of being viewed as better than others fits into this category.

The ScrumMaster's Role

The ScrumMaster's role is to educate the team about the four toxins and then coach them so they are able to identify the toxins in real time, and make each other accountable for not using the toxins. You'll be surprised how often these toxins are present in your discussions and how just raising awareness of them can be helpful. Communication becomes nicer, and you will be able to reach agreement much more quickly. The overall environment will be less like a thunderstorm, and overall motivation and ownership will increase. Teams working in a less toxic environment have more fun, and that's what you are looking for, right?

Exercise: Team Toxins

Which team toxins are the most common in your team?

- ☐ Blame
- ☐ Defensiveness
- ☐ Stonewalling
- ☐ Contempt

What are the most common situations in which you face them?

_____

_____

_____

FOCUS ON RESPONSIBILITY

One of the most critical parts of the Agile mindset and of Scrum culture is responsibility. Everybody talks about responsibility, but not many of us take full responsibility in every situation. Christopher Avery [14] has created a very nice responsibility model that explains how responsibility works. During the long years of evolution, people's brains were trained to be quick in decision making. Whenever even a small issue emerged, the brain would offer an option for how to approach it. As an example, imagine you are parking your car in an underground garage and you accidentally scratch the car next to you.

Denial

The first solution your brain will offer is denial. "This never even happened. I don't see any scratches, the car is just dirty. And the sound? It was only sand crunching."

Back at your Scrum team, it could turn up as pretending that a piece of code works, even if it just crashed. "It's coded, so it works."

Laying Blame

While you are not fine with denial, your brain will offer the next possible solution of laying blame in no time. "It's his fault! If he had parked straight, this would never have happened."

In the Scrum environment this could be pointing at the Product Owner because he described something wrong, or it could be the fault of another team member. "I coded it right; it's his fault that it's not working."

Justify

Still not happy? Don't worry, your brain is proposing another resolution. You can justify it. "It happens. Everyone scratches a car from time to time, right? And those underground parking spots are so narrow."

The Scrum team, at the beginning of their journey, uses this excuse quite often when trying to explain why they can't plan a Sprint or didn't finish with the Sprint results they expected. "Anything can happen during the Sprint, so we can't guarantee anything. In software development we often encounter technical difficulties, right? That's just the way it is."

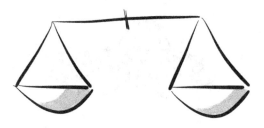

Shame

If you still don't feel good about it, you can see it as your own fault. "It's all my fault. I will never learn how to park in those narrow spaces."

The Scrum team may express their frustration over the lack of cross-functionality and say, "We don't have enough experience in that product part. It's too difficult. It would take us years to learn it." They usually don't mind that they are in fact saying, "We are not good enough," and they are trying to hide it by claiming that it's normal to ask for experts.

Obligation

So what's next? Solve it as if it is your obligation. "I've left my business card behind the wiper blade. It's my duty to do this. The insurance will cover it."

This stage reminds me of a Scrum team that follows Scrum just because they have to. Someone told them to have meetings, so they have them without understanding. "We do Standup because of Scrum—we have to. It's one of the Scrum meetings, isn't it?"

Quit

At any time you can decide to quit. "I'm not going to solve it; it's not important for me." No one is forcing you to be responsible. However, don't trick yourself. None of the previous levels is real responsibility. And nothing previously mentioned helps you prevent those things from happening in the future.

Responsibility

When you decide to take responsibility, this is the final level of the responsibility process model. It starts with a question: "What can I do differently next time so it will not happen to me in the future?" In this example, it could be anything starting from the use of public transport instead, parking in a street where there is more space, buying parking sensors, attending a specific driving class, or practicing with cardboard boxes.

To give you an example from the Scrum team, real responsibility is when a bug is reported and the team not only fixes it but in addition discusses what they will change next time so it will not be repeated. Another example might be impediments. An immature team expects someone to remove these, whereas the good team takes over the activity and comes up with some way of improving it.

ORGANIZATION AS A TRIBE

Another interesting concept from the theory of building teams comes from the book *Tribal Leadership* [15]. To give you a taste of this concept, every organization consists of tribes. A tribe is a group of people who know each other. When they reach out to other tribe members somewhere, they say hello. The tribe can be as big as about 150 people; bigger companies consist of tribal networks.

Each tribe has a different culture. However, every organization has some dominant tribal culture according to which it can be classified. Such a culture then shapes people's behavior and approach.

As in the other models, you can't skip stages. In addition, every stage needs a different leadership style to support the people in their tribal leadership development. Last but not least, it's quite common that tribes are temporarily dragged one stage down when under stress. And because every change brings a certain level of stress, Agile transformation usually initiates such a tribal stage movement.

Stage 1: Life Sucks

The first level of tribal leadership is not very common in Agile or even in the IT environment as a whole. We see it in street gangs and prisons. Overall, we observe such cultures in about 2% of companies worldwide.

The "Life sucks" culture is about individuals who have lost all hope. They are alone and other people just don't get it. Life itself sucks.

Stage 2: My Life Sucks

Wow, what an improvement to say, "My life sucks." People in such tribes complain a lot. They are far away from taking any responsibility. It's about passivity, disconnection, disengagement, and cynicism. You can hear various complaints—"My life sucks because the product is crap, I have an idiotic boss, I have to drive two hours to work, and the coffee is not good." Such tribes are dominant in 25% of companies worldwide.

In Agile environments it's quite common to be drawn into this stage during the initial phase of Agile transformation. And you often see it in the "Scrum-but" cultures as well. "My life sucks because I have to do Scrum."

To help people get out of this swamp, encourage them, elevate their self-confidence, and make them successful so they have the courage to take a more positive point of view. Only people who experience personal success are ready for the next tribal stage.

Steps toward the Next Stage

- Empower individuals so they believe they can make it. Give them a chance to shine.
- Give them more responsibility and encourage them to take ownership.
- Generate fast wins to increase self-confidence.

Stage 3: I'm Great (but You Are Not)

This is the typical world environment. It's a culture of specialization, experts, and absolutely necessary people who keep their know-how and information to themselves. It's the dominant form for 49% of companies worldwide. It's comfortable. It feels good because the people are finally successful (whereas others are not). And now, we are going to break this individualistic cult and build some team self-organization and responsibility. How can that possibly work?

Nonetheless, we can't forget that this stage is necessary as a middle step for people coming from "My life sucks" cultures. Only confident people who believe in their skills and abilities can create a great team. Every individual first needs to experience his own success in order to transcend it in favor of the team next time.

This stage is about personal accomplishments, the importance of job titles, and the feeling that "I'm putting in more than others": "I'm good at my job, I try harder than others, and I'm more skillful than most." The position of Senior ScrumMaster comes from this environment, and most of the managers who have teams at Stage 2 are at this level.

A ScrumMaster at Stage 3 underestimates his team; for example, "I'm a great ScrumMaster, but my team is not as good. They are demotivated and lazy. I don't trust them to work as hard as me." It's not necessary to mention that such a person is not a great ScrumMaster. As for common team examples, they could be like this: "They [the other team members] don't understand reporting, so I have to do all the work concerning reports. It would have taken years for them to learn it."

Step toward the Next Stage

- Let the team experience success. Once they realize their personal dream of being successful, they are ready for the next stage.

Stage 4: We Are Great

Finally, there is a stage where "We are great" is the statement the tribe lives by. It's a tribe dominant in 22% of companies worldwide, and it's quite a positive environment to be in. It's a culture of ownership, responsibility, and cooperation.

People in such environments are usually proud of working in their company and happy to recommend it to their friends. They believe in their product and have one goal, rather than competing with each other.

Once you adopt Agile and become not just a group of coworkers but a real team as defined in Scrum, you realize that you are at this stage. Teams are less self-centric and start to turn outside. People say, "We are great, and we are ready to share pieces of our culture with others." They offer help and experience, but at the same time they long for new learning.

However, even Agile and Scrum are not miraculous methods for cultivating the "We are great" culture. If you don't give people enough space to shine as individuals and appreciate them enough first, they will most likely not be ready for true Agile culture, and Scrum will fail. Remember, you can't skip the stages. It will not work.

Remember

- Team success is more important than individual appraisals.
- The competitiveness of the environment in general is much lower.
- We are great and we are ready to help others to become even greater.

Stage 5: Life Is Great

The last stage of the tribal leadership model continues in the same vein. The competitiveness of the environment is decreasing. This group is going to make history. "We are not at war with our competitors. We are at war with cancer" was one of the replies from those interviewed for the *Tribal Leadership* book [15]. It's the dominant stage for only 2% of companies worldwide, and it's breaking some general patterns on which the last century's management was built. In order to be there, you must be a bit wacky. Some Agile coaches are working at this level. They are *changing the way companies work*. They don't look upon other Agile coaches as competitors because, despite the different business affiliations, they share the same goal.

We all try to change the overall industry or even the world to be more Agile, so why should we compete with each other? If we support each other instead, the market will grow, and there will be enough work for all of us. But indeed, not every Agile person would agree, so there are still enough people who take it personally. But it's a good example to share.

Exercise: Tribal Leadership Stages

Which tribes can you see in your organization? Which one is dominant?

- ☐ Life sucks.
- ☐ My life sucks.
- ☐ I'm great (and you are not).
- ☐ We are great.
- ☐ Life is great.

What can you do to help people move to the next stage?

_____

_____

_____

CHOOSE THE RIGHT LEADERSHIP STYLE

Another concept that is useful to apply at the enterprise level was originally described in David Marquet's book *Turn the Ship Around* [16]. David was the captain of a US Navy submarine and applied this new leadership approach. Bear this in mind before you say it will never work in your company.

Leader-Follower

Traditional management in companies works on the so-called leader-follower model. The manager (leader) is the most knowledgeable person who is supposed to give orders to workers and is responsible for planning, allocation of resources, and overall people organization. It used to be the only model in companies during the twentieth century. And in some environments it worked well. However, the more creative and unpredictable the business was, the less convenient and efficient such a leadership style turned out to be.

Leader-Leader

The opposite approach is the leader-leader model, where we believe that the people at each level can solve most of their problems by themselves. We don't give many orders anymore but encourage them to come up with solutions and take over responsibility for running the company. To be clear, I'm not saying we don't need any managers. I'm suggesting that we change our management style.

Looking at this concept from the ScrumMaster's point of view, that's exactly what each ScrumMaster has to do—implement the leader-leader model and build leaders in the organization, not just followers.

Remember

- Innovative environments need to involve people in the decision-making process.
- Enforce the leader-leader model across the organization.

USE DECENTRALIZATION

One aspect of creating a successful self-organized team is the ability to use decentralization techniques. As opposed to the centrally controlled hierarchy of the traditional process-oriented structures, modern organizations exploit the advantages of various decentralization techniques to involve the team in creating processes, enhancing their ownership, and supporting creativity. We often use *diverge-merge* techniques to have efficient discussions and share ideas among people.

The following sections describe recommendations for decentralization techniques.

Book Club

How much time have you spent with your colleagues, learning with each other? Try organizing a book club. You can read a book or watch a video together and then discuss what you found interesting or learned from it. This should be a group activity, not a presentation by an individual who has read the book or seen the film.

Travelers

Teams should be as stable and fixed as possible. However, sometimes you might need to have some *travelers* who can freely move across the organization and help any team that accepts their help. It's great for sharing know-how, bringing new points of view, and breaking down the status quo.

Review Bazaar

Instead of a Sprint Review meeting, you can organize it as a Review Bazaar [17] where teams present their results and, in the meantime, team members walk around and visit other people's exhibitions. It's faster and much more fun.

Experiment Board

Conduct experiments and make them visible to everyone at the company. Share goals, assumptions, and results. Create a physical Experiment Board so everyone can see it, get inspired, and try their own creative ideas.

Open Space

The open-space format doesn't have to be dedicated to unconferences; you can benefit from it within your company as well. Agile companies organize open spaces regularly every month or quarter.

When your company is willing to allow people to spend their time on such open-format events without a clear up-front agenda, it's truly Agile.

How To

- Start with the marketplace where participants design their agenda.
- Continue with free parallel discussions; feel free to move to a different group if you are not sufficiently interested.
- Finish with a joint summary from the sessions.
- Check the open-space rules before you organize your own [18,19].

World Café

Another common decentralized workshop format companies often use to involve more people and let them discuss and self-organize is the world-café format [20].

How To

- Introduce a theme and let everyone focus and concentrate for a minute.
- Put up the initial question and let groups discuss it.
- Keep one person at each table to introduce the results to newcomers and let others mix and find a new group.
- Repeat the last two steps three times for slightly different questions.
- Present a summary to the group.

6

· · ·

IMPLEMENTING CHANGE

Every change is difficult. It brings resistance, fear, and uncertainty.
"Will I still be successful in the new environment? Can I adapt
to the new way of working fast enough? Will I like it?" The great
ScrumMaster is aware of those factors, creates a safe environment
for people affected by the change, and gives them a hand to help
them cross the edge of the change.

GO FOR A CHANGE

Before changing the way you work, it's good to clarify why you want to do it. Doing it just because it's something new is not enough. What are the current bottlenecks and strengths, and what are you expecting? If the expectation is not high enough, you may not be ready for a change yet; before you move on and start with Agile, you must have a better reason than you read about it in a newspaper. The Agile Wheel is a useful exercise to help you decide if it's the right time for the change or not and why.

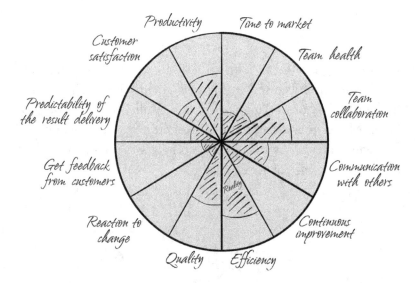

The wheel consists of the most important reasons for adopting Agile. It can be used as an assessment tool in a group or by individuals. It's a great way to start a wider discussion across the company, department, or team. You don't have to agree on numbers. It's more for initiating a conversation, visualizing a different point of view.

How does it work? First, identify reality—how do you feel about each segment? The middle of the circle stands for "not good: ☹" and the edges stand for "great: ☺."

Once you have determined your current state, look at it from a different perspective and assess your expectations—where would you like to be in six months? See the following example.

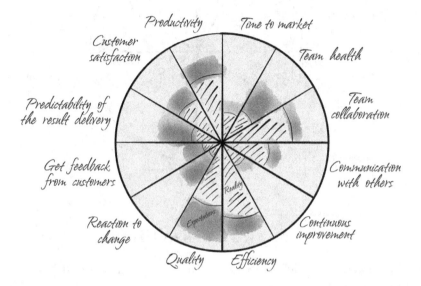

Exercise: Agile Wheel

Examine your current state and your expectations from change in the following categories and draw the Agile Wheel for your situation and context.

Consider:

How similar/different are the individual wheels of all the team members?

Understand why, and have a conversation about it.

Discuss which actions you are going to take based on that discussion.

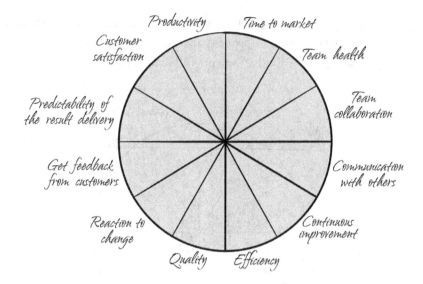

CHANGE BEHAVIOR

Implementing Agile and Scrum means a big change. And Scrum-Masters should act as the organization's guides to take it through the change. There are two concepts that are particularly important for ScrumMasters to understand about change. The first one comes from the ORSC framework [4] and describes change as an edge: "The Edge is the line between the known and the unknown—it is at the limit of what we know about ourselves. Any time you try a new behavior or idea or perspective, you are crossing an Edge. As long as teams and individuals grow and change, there will always be new frontiers and edges to explore" [21].

Every change consists of several smaller edges to be crossed on the way, and the role of the ScrumMaster is to understand those edges and help individuals, teams, and organizations to cross them. Also, different people and parts of organizations will see different challenges to overcome.

Keeping this in mind, the most applicable approach from the ScrumMaster State of Mind model would be coaching. As a good guide, the ScrumMaster should offer a hand and help people over the top whenever they are ready, but not push them over.

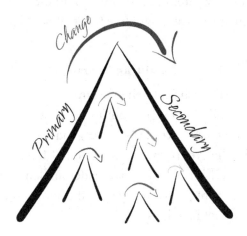

EIGHT STEPS FOR SUCCESSFUL CHANGE

The second important concept about change management describes a process for implementing successful change in eight steps [22]. It addresses those change phases. First, you set the stage. Next, you decide what to do and make it happen. And finally, you make it stick.

Create a Sense of Urgency

The very first step before you implement any change is to create a sense of urgency. Make the change necessary, because until you feel pain in your current processes, there is no need for improvement. And it doesn't matter if the desired change is huge, like

an Agile transformation, or small, like using Git instead of CVS. Without good motivation and a good reason there will be no change. Be honest and transparent in presenting both the opportunities and the threats; otherwise you might lose the trust of others.

Guiding Team

As one individual, it's hard to change anyone. You should focus on early adopters and encourage them to become part of your team. You need people who are passionate, good communicators, and leaders. Make the group diverse. It shouldn't follow any organizational structures if it is to access a broader audience. In general, if there are three of you, you already have the ability to create a snowball effect by attracting others.

Change Vision

Creating a change vision and strategy is another important part of your change process. There are thousands of great ideas about what can be done. However, you should present the change clearly and simply so people understand it. Be sure all your change team members can explain it in less than five minutes.

Think about the real goal you would like to achieve—which is unlikely to be Agile (which is a strategy for achieving a goal). Your goal is more likely to be more flexibility, increased quality, and improved customer satisfaction.

Understanding and Buy-in

And now comes the hard part. Regardless of how great your vision is or how much you believe in it, you have to sell it to others. And others have various fears; their contexts are different, and the way change impacts them will also be different. So all you need here are good listening skills, an understanding of their context, and the ability to fill them with enthusiasm. You will also need patience, because it takes some people longer to buy into a new idea. Also, don't be frustrated by repeating your vision over and over again. It takes time for each piece of information about a change to sink in.

Empower Others to Act

This part of change management is usually quite close to what ScrumMasters do. To empower others to act, you need to remove impediments so that you can make it easier for them to change. The ability to build self-organized teams is extremely helpful here.

It's not only about removing what is blocking others but about acknowledgment and recognition of people who have taken some steps toward change.

Short-Term Wins

Demonstrate success frequently. It's great to have a long-term vision and a challenging goal. However, you need milestones to celebrate along the way. Make them simple so you can celebrate success early enough to increase overall positivity. "It's challenging and sometimes even exhausting, but we are going to make it."

You will need to reflect upon and adapt your strategy because no change can be planned in detail up front. So "dance in the moment." Be transparent about the failures. If you try to hide the failures, you will only risk making them grow into gossip, which can possibly destroy your change effort.

Don't Let Up

Some changes fail just because they are declared as *done* too early, when people are still somewhere on the way to the desired state.

And as their new positions haven't stuck yet, they usually—sooner or later—revert to their old habits.

Such an early victory seems to be good motivation, but in the long term it usually destroys the whole change. "From now, we are already Agile." The team usually reacts with irony, saying, "We are already Agile now, so we don't need to change anymore."

So does it mean that after a certain stage we don't need to change and try hard anymore? Not quite. Perfection is not a state, it's a journey. So you will never be finished. Changes never stop. The goal can be extended and adapted, but there is never an end.

Create a New Culture

Finally, the last step is to make it stick. Make the new way of working an integral part of your culture. That's the way we are. And there is no discussion about it.

As people slowly accept new ways of working, you might hear something they would never have said before as if it's the most natural thing:

> "We are not going to follow any detailed plan; we want to be invited to create it and change it based on feedback."

> "We are not here just to write code; we need real customer feedback to understand customers and make them happy."

Hints for Great ScrumMasters

- Understand team dynamics. Distinguish among a group of individuals, a good team, and a great team.
- Dysfunctions need to be fixed before the team can emerge.
- Toxins prevent your team from flourishing.
- Every change is hard; before you change anything, you must have a good reason and high motivation.
- Resistance is a common change behavior; don't push too much.
- The great ScrumMaster is a leader who creates new leaders out of the people around him.

7
. . .

THE SCRUMMASTER'S TOOLBOX

In the everyday life of the great ScrumMaster, he needs to understand and use many tools. Let's start with understanding how people become masters.

MASTERING SHU HA RI

Japanese culture is quite inspiring. One of the ideas the Agile community took from Japanese martial arts is the concept of mastering Shu Ha Ri [23].

In Shu, we repeat the forms and discipline ourselves so that our bodies absorb the forms that our forebears created. We remain faithful to these forms with no deviation. Next, in the stage of Ha, once we have disciplined ourselves to acquire the forms and movements, we make innovations. In this process the forms may be broken and discarded. Finally, in Ri, we completely depart from the forms, open the door to creative technique, and arrive in a place where we act in accordance with what our heart/mind desires, unhindered while not overstepping laws [24].

Shu

Shu is the initial stage where people get the basics by following the instructions of one teacher. It's the drill stage, where people repeat the individual practices over and over again. It's like what soldiers go through in the army. You are not finished until all the practices have become second nature to you, like walking or breathing, so you don't have to think about them before applying them.

In the Shu stage of Scrum implementation, the team should focus on the drill of individual practices, for example, "How shall we do planning?" and "How should we write User Stories?"

What to Do

- Drill individual practices.
- Follow recommendations.
- Don't give up; it works the way it is described.
- Be patient; it will take time to train your muscle memory.

Ha

The second level of mastering is called Ha. Because all the practices are already learned and absorbed into muscle memory, at this stage you start to dig into the purpose. Based on that deep understanding, people are able to detach their particular application and combine the advice from several teachers/directions.

In the Ha stage of Scrum implementation the team should focus on answering questions like "What is behind those practices? How does Scrum work from a psychological perspective? How do those parts influence each other?"

What to Do

- Inspect and adapt, create your own deviations, but keep the original meaning and philosophy.
- Go for deep understanding of purpose.
- Think about practices, concepts, and frameworks in context, how they support or contradict each other.

Ri

Finally, in the last stage people are not learning from others but from their own practical application and experience. They build on the background they gained through Shu and the deep understanding gained through Ha. They eventually become teachers and create their own concepts and practices.

In the Ri stage of Scrum implementation the team starts thinking about applying Scrum in areas other than software development, such as marketing, sales, operations, call centers, or in their private lives.

What to Do

- Learn from your own practice and experience.
- Develop and share new concepts, and teach others.

Application

The Shu Ha Ri concept is especially important for ScrumMasters because they need to recognize the stage the team has reached and adjust their approach accordingly. The following situation is quite common:

The team has passed training and the first few Sprints. Some practices are not so easy for them to embrace—for example, Standups—so they suggest doing them less frequently or abandoning them altogether.

Nonetheless, such teams cannot just skip the Shu and Ha phases and move directly into Ri without a solid grounding. Such shortcuts never create masters, just overconfident people who pretend they are masters.

Passing through each of the Shu Ha Ri phases takes time (often years), so be patient. Remember that even simple things like walking, running, or cycling took time for you to master when you were young.

Exercise: Shu Ha Ri

In which state is your team now?

- ☐ Shu
- ☐ Ha
- ☐ Ri

What do they need to understand or practice?

_____

_____

_____

SYSTEM RULE

As was mentioned before, the great ScrumMaster must work at the system level. And one of the core elements of success at this level is to believe that "everyone is right, but only partially" [25]. This simple statement will help you to believe that each voice is worth listening to. At the system level you don't take sides; it's not about deciding who is right or wrong. Every statement someone makes is just a signal from the whole system that is trying to attract your attention. Especially during changes and transformations, whole systems can become frustrated, frightened, or uncomfortable. It is the same with individuals. And the role of the ScrumMaster is to coach the overall system in order to find balance and stability again.

The great ScrumMaster is always searching for different kinds of signals so he can reflect them back to the system like a mirror. Such signals can be pretty much anything you can sense. They could be people who are complaining, angry, or frustrated; people who are quiet at meetings or who point fingers at each other instead of accepting responsibility; or people who seek reasons for why a problem can't be solved. Every one of these can be reflected back to the system if you believe that in each of these signals there is some portion of the truth.

Everyone is right... only partially.

Example: Improvements

Let's imagine that you've just joined a new Scrum team as Scrum-Master. They are supposed to be good given what the managers have said, and the team members confirm this when you ask them.

However, the system sends signals that suggest the opposite. There is no real discussion at the meetings, their Retrospective lacks any deeper understanding, and no improvements are coming from it. They don't complain, but they are not a great Scrum team either.

Such a scenario is actually quite common. You just need to be sensitive to the signals coming from the system—in this case, artificial harmony and the absence of deeper discussion—and reflect this back to the team so they can realize what's happening and change.

Example: Product Owner

Another example could be a team that is not willing to present the product at Sprint Review.

You will hear voices from the system saying, "Developers are not good at presentations" and "The Product Owner should give the presentation because he is the one who decided that this functionality should be done." Before you start teaching team members how to make such a presentation or, with irritation in your voice, tell them they have to present because of the Scrum, think about what you can do about it at the system level and what exactly the system is trying to say.

Maybe they are not good at presenting, or maybe the Product Owner is not part of the team and as a consequence they don't believe in the product. And they are partially right, but there is a bigger picture as well. You just need to reveal it to the system so they can adjust accordingly, as a team.

Example: Frustration

The team is at the beginning of the Agile and Scrum transformation when usually the biggest challenge is to understand and apply cross-functionality.

Imagine a person expressing his frustration in rather a strange way, but that's what people under stress do, right? At the Standup he

says, "I have no work in the Sprint, so I didn't do anything yesterday, and I'm not going to do anything today either. No impediments."

You might be angry about him, and other team members might be inclined to laugh, but the only thing you heard was the voice of the system saying, "There is something wrong! Help us!" And if you suppress your anger and display curiosity instead, you might find out that that voice is just a symptom of a deeper root cause that, in this particular case, could be that they are a group of individuals who work according to their specializations and who mostly don't understand Backlog Items, and so they are completely lost. They have tried to communicate that they can't imagine how Scrum would work for them a thousand times already, but no one listened to them.

So they are partially right. Scrum is not for them now. They would have to change the way they work in order to make it work. And that's exactly what the ScrumMaster has to do—understand those signals and help the system to realize they are the only ones who can fix it. In this case, it's about explaining not only what they should do but why they should do it and guiding them through the whole process of change.

POSITIVITY

Positivity is a crucial aspect of every successful system or individual. It works for both business and in private life. Based on the positivity ratio, John Gottman did experiments on marital and relationship stability with very high accuracy, and later on Marcial Losada used the same negativity-to-positivity ratio for business teams. Their results were surprisingly consistent.

Every great system should contain about three to five positive events to one negative. So if you as ScrumMaster keep the positivity high, you are halfway to achieving your goal.

When a human system contains 3 to 5x as much positivity as negativity, it is significantly more likely to thrive [26].

A ratio of 3.0 to 6.0 has been found to be highly correlated with high performance [27].

The team with five times more positive than negative events is significantly more likely to be successful [28].

How to Increase Positivity

Here are some easy ways to increase positivity:

- **Use a Retrospective to increase positivity.** Never talk only about issues. Spend a significant amount of time on things that were great and that you would like to keep or do more of. Instead of repeating plus and delta, make up something more creative like drawing a boat together. One of my favorite Retrospective formats is asking what makes the team smile about the last Sprint, instead of using the traditional plus.
- **Look at the issues from the bright side.** Every glass can be either half full or half empty. It's the same with events that happen to your team.

- **Visualize positive events and celebrate success.** Create a "positivity wall." Don't miss any opportunity to celebrate. Our team members brought cake to the demo from time to time. And on other occasions we went out for drinks to celebrate after work.
- **Don't panic.** Even if the situation seems to be hard, increase positivity and smile ☺.

FACILITATION

Facilitation is the core practice of every ScrumMaster. So let's look at how to be a better facilitator. First of all, facilitation means defining the frame and flow of a discussion, not the content. It's a structured process for running a communication, but not a rigid one that follows the same plan in any situation. The good facilitator should be flexible and ready to change his agenda.

What are the attitudes or behaviors of a great facilitator? He must be good at listening and hear everyone's voice, increase positivity, be flexible, and use his intuition, but not be too attached to a single idea. The facilitator must sense the level of energy in the room and adjust the format accordingly. He must come prepared, but he must be flexible and have neither a fixed structure nor a fixed plan.

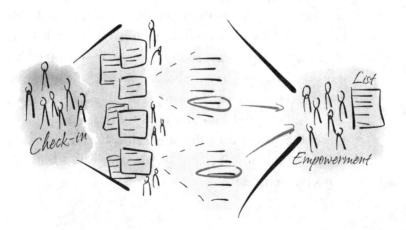

What to Do

- The facilitator is responsible for the container, not the content.
- He defines a clear purpose and deliverables for each meeting before starting.
- He reviews the meeting's purpose and outcome with the participants.
- He opens the meeting with a strong start.
- He does a check-in activity at the beginning and at the end of the meeting.
- He explains and uses the parking lot.
- He is not too attached to his plan. If it happens not to be working, he adapts it to the situation or the team's needs.
- He expands and narrows the space to improve people's understanding and get all their different opinions.

Before the Meeting

Before every meeting the facilitator must make sure there is a clear purpose—why the meeting was organized. Make it SMART (specific, measurable, achievable, and agreed, realistic, timed). If there is no purpose, don't run the meeting.

Once you have that, think about what deliverables the meeting should produce in order to make it successful. Deliverables are of three kinds:

- **Heads**—anything you can learn, such as skills, ideas, status updates
- **Hearts**—to get buy-in, belief, engagement, or excitement
- **Hands**—to create some tangible output, such as action plans, timelines, or lists

Finally, think about who needs to be involved, when and where the meeting will take place, and how you will facilitate it.

During the Meeting

The first minutes of the meeting are crucial, and the facilitator should open with a strong start. Think about the energy level, the engagement. Always share the meeting's purpose, expected deliverables, and agenda for review by the audience. Let them think about what's in it for them.

During the meeting the facilitator uses several tools, like brainstorming, listing and grouping, prioritization, or working in pairs or groups, to expand the space or narrow it and closes the meeting with the expected outcome.

At the end of the meeting, don't forget to summarize the meeting; review how the group addressed the purpose and summarize the action items.

Example: Retrospective

In the following example there is a preparation sheet for the facilitation of one of the most common Scrum meetings. The example shows the application of the facilitation theory described previously. How you facilitate a Retrospective may differ based on the team, the situation, and other factors.

Before the meeting

- Purpose:
  - Continuous improvement of our processes
- Deliverables:
  - Understanding of the current state
  - Engagement and willingness to take over responsibility
  - Clear action items to be done during the next Sprint
- Who:
  - Development team and Product Owner
- When:
  - At the end of the Sprint
- Duration:
  - 1 hour

During the meeting

1. Start the retrospective with a check-in activity to engage the participants and get their creativity started, for example, with a weather check-in: "If you were the weather, what kind of weather would you be?" [1 minute]

2. Explain the format of the meeting and review the purpose and deliverables. Create a parking lot for additional ideas that are not part of the meeting. [2 minutes]

3. Expand the space. Let the team identify the areas to be discussed. You can use delta and plus or a star with stickers. [5 minutes]

4. Narrow the space by asking the team to group similar areas together and give them a label. [3 minutes]

5. Use dot voting to establish priorities. [1 minute]

6. For the most important area, expand the space again by generating options. Use root-cause analysis or brainstorming to get new ideas.

7. Narrow the space by letting the team select a few action items for the next Sprint.

8. Repeat the last two steps until you have nearly filled the given time frame.

9. Close the session by reviewing the action items.

Do a check-in activity to close the meeting with one word, such as "Express in one word what this Retrospective gave you."

COACHING

Coaching is one of the most important skills of every ScrumMaster. Coaching means evoking self-awareness and self-realization. It helps people come up with creative solutions and identify goals for their own development. Unlike mentoring, coaching is not about sharing experiences, teaching, or advising.

> Unlocking a person's potential to maximize their own performance. It is helping them to learn rather than teaching them [29].

> Coaching is partnering with clients in a thought-provoking and creative process that inspires them to maximize their personal and professional potential [30].

Coaching is not limited to individuals but can be successfully applied to teams, groups, and organizations. While coaching at the team or organization level, the coach focuses more on Relationship Systems Intelligence. "Beyond Emotional Intelligence (relationship with oneself) and Social Intelligence (relationship with others) is the realm of Relationship Systems Intelligence where one's focus shifts to the relationship with the group, team or system" [4]. This particular coaching model is especially useful for ScrumMasters to help the organization grow.

How do you become a coach? Focus on your listening skills: don't give advice but help people come up with their own solutions. As a coach you can't get too involved. The team you coach should invent their own solutions. Your only task is to adjust a mirror to increase their awareness and allow them to come up with new points of view.

The fundamental technique of coaching is the ability to ask good questions to initiate the thinking process. They should not be asked with the *right answer* in mind. The questions that increase people's awareness and start the thinking process are always open-ended questions that are likely to be met with longer answers—not yes/no replies.

Powerful Questions

There are many powerful questions you can use during a coaching conversation. Here is a list of my favorites:

- What would you like to achieve/change/get?
- What is important to you now?
- What would your perfect Standup look like?
- What is working well?
- What progress have you made so far?
- What would you have to change in order to achieve your goal?
- What can you do about it?
- What can you do differently?

- What do you need to stop doing?
- What else?
- What's next?

Exercise: Powerful Questions

Practice your skill of asking powerful questions. Write down a few you would like to use next time. Use my questions or any online reference, for example, coactive.com [31] or coaching cards from the Agile Coaching Institute [32].

_____

_____

_____

ROOT-CAUSE ANALYSIS

As a ScrumMaster, you can either treat symptoms, and always be too busy, or learn how to identify the cause of a problem. It's the difference between reactive and proactive approaches. In the first one, you get so tired of combating the fire that you have no energy to attack it at its source, whereas in the other you take your time after the fire is out, stop cleaning up, and find a solution to fix the root cause of the problem so it will never happen again.

A typical example could be bugs. In the traditional world, you focus all your effort on fixing them. In the Agile environment we also fix them, but more importantly we address the root cause in the application, for example, write an automated test to prevent problems or adjust our process and do pair programming or review.

Most of the root-cause analysis literature describes a complex process of identifying the cause, but in most cases it's not necessary. You can try the following simple concepts and see if they help you to better understand the problem.

Note

- Every team or organization is like an organism, and it can become "ill."
- Don't concentrate on treating symptoms only.
- Focus on healing the cause of the illness instead, and you will eliminate several symptoms at once.
- Choose a proactive approach instead of a reactive one.

Fishbone

One of the most common forms of root-cause analysis is called fishbone or Ishikawa. There are several ways to design it, but the most common is asking what, where, when, who, and why something is happening. It helps you to look at the problem from different angles and identify the root cause.

Example: Predictability

We are not predictable. We never know when the release will be ready.

"**What** makes us unpredictable?"

"We have changes coming through all the time."

"**Where** do the changes come from?"

"Usually from the CEO, who is the visionary of the product, and a bit from our users, but those are usually minor changes."

"**When** is the most critical time?"

"When marketing wants insights in order to prepare campaigns and forces us to commit to a certain functionality several Sprints before the product launch."

"**Who** can influence that?"

"Our CEO, who might be more present during the release and make his comments at every Sprint Review."

"**Why** is he not present at each Sprint Review?"

"He joined the first few reviews, but we didn't deliver much functionality at that time, so he gradually stopped coming. Maybe it's time to invite him again."

Five Whys

The second most common root-cause analysis tool is called Five Whys. The usage is quite simple. In order to identify the true root cause, ask "Why?" five times.

Example: Low Quality

Our product has low quality. We have too many bugs.

"**Why** do you have so many bugs?"

"Because we don't test."

"**Why** don't you test?"

"We do test in some cases, but because the system is very complex, we can't understand how every possible scenario works."

"**Why** don't you understand it?"

"We don't know how the users are using the system."

"**Why** don't you know how the users are using the system?"

"We've never seen our users or asked them for feedback."

"**Why** have you never asked them for feedback?"

"Because we thought it was the Product Owner's job to do it."

IMPACT MAPPING

Impact mapping [6] is usually mentioned in relation to product development. However, it's quite a useful technique in any strategic planning on organizational change, Agile adoption, or Scrum implementation.

> Impact mapping is a strategic planning technique that prevents organisations from getting lost while building products and delivering projects, by clearly communicating assumptions, helping teams align their activities with overall business objectives and making better roadmap decisions [33].

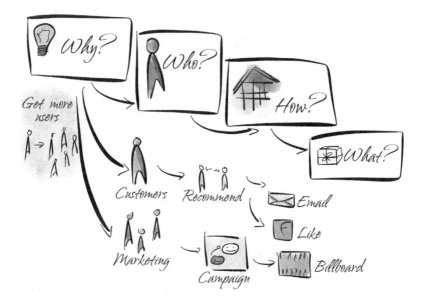

Impact mapping is a creative technique whereby you create a mind map in answer to the following questions:

"Why are we doing this?"

Start with a **goal**. It should be SMART: specific, measurable, achievable, and agreed, realistic, and timed.

"Who can produce the desired effect?"

Focus on **actors**—who can support you and who can obstruct the desired effect? Who will be impacted by it?

"How should our actors' behavior change?"

Investigate the actors' **impact**—how the actors from the previous step can help you to achieve the goal or prevent you from achieving success.

"What can we do to support the impact?"

Think about the desired outcome and deliverables. What can you do to make them happen?

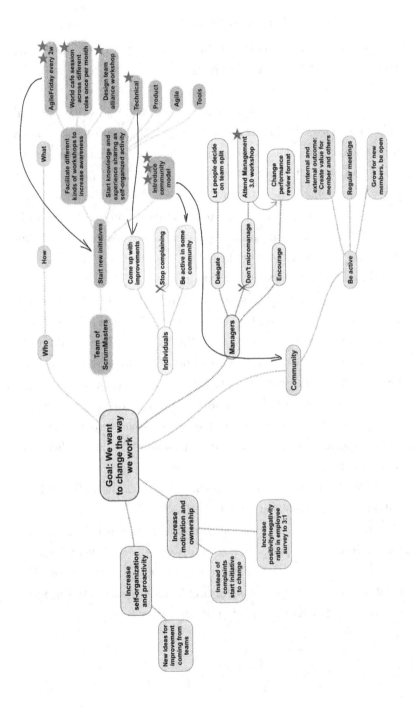

Example: Impact Mapping

Imagine you work for a company that has already implemented Agile principles and Scrum. As ScrumMaster, your job is to improve the culture, empower people, increase motivation, and boost proactivity.

Using the impact mapping technique, you start with your goal definition. Don't be too hasty. The first goal that springs to mind is unlikely to be the right one. Think about something valuable, something you would be proud to achieve. And make it measurable so you can recognize when it's done (see the left part of the mind map).

The next step is to think about actors—who can help you to achieve your goal of a proactive, positive, and motivated environment. In this example you started with a team of ScrumMasters, individual team members, and managers.

Now let's look at how you want them to change their approach—so, for example, ScrumMasters should start new initiatives and not be preoccupied with the team and its impediments. As for managers, you want them to stop micromanaging the team because that's really damaging to your culture, and so forth.

The next level is looking at what you can do to support the desired effect—for example, organize an Agile Friday session to share experiences, introduce the community model to the company, and so on.

Once you are finished, you can do star voting on the individual options regarding the expected impact.

As a next step, think about how those actions influence your map. Some can support other actions; some may do the opposite.

Finally, be aware that such a mind map is never done. You have to update it regularly according to the organization's progress or any other environmental changes in the company.

SCALING SCRUM

One of the most common questions is how to adopt Scrum when there are bigger products and more teams. Scaling Scrum frameworks suggest many approaches. I believe the easier, the better. Scrum itself is a very simple empirical process with few rules, roles, and meetings, so why should we scale it in a rigid process way? Therefore, my choice is clearly a Large-Scale Scrum framework— LeSS. It's simple, and it applies Scrum to scaling. As Craig Larman and Bas Vodde wrote, "Since 2005, we've worked with clients to apply the LeSS (Large-Scale Scrum) framework for scaling Scrum, lean and agile development to big product groups. We share that experience and knowledge through LeSS so that you too can succeed when scaling" [34].

Let's start with the most important aspect of LeSS. Regardless of how big your product is, there is still only one Product Owner and one Product Backlog. If you implement it in this way, you force the company to look at your product from the business perspective, not from the viewpoint of technical or architectural structure. Such a Product Owner never works alone, but it's important to have only one head to decide on functionality and priorities. In addition, LeSS divides planning into two phases and adds an overall Retrospective to improve product group communication and cooperation. There are still cross-functional development teams with ScrumMasters, and most of the other artifacts are the same as with one-product and one-team implementation.

LeSS is quite a simple framework that works well in different corporate environments. I won't go into the details here; there are many published case studies on LeSS application [35].

The LeSS framework focuses not only on how to organize product development but also on how to apply it at the organizational

level, including Lean thinking, system thinking, go-see principles, management role, and overall company organization.

KANBAN INSIGHT SCRUM CHECKLIST

It has never been a question of Scrum *or* Kanban. It has always been both. Kanban is an integral part of Scrum. It's Scrum's spice. Without it, Scrum would not be so great. Let's see how infected you are by Kanban:

- ☐ **Visualization**
  - ☐ Scrum Board
  - ☐ Avatars for team members
  - ☐ Different card colors
  - ☐ Making dots for tasks not done within one day
  - ☐ Charter/story map/impact map visible on walls
  - ☐ Top priorities of the Product Backlog visible on walls
- ☐ **Kaizen**
  - ☐ You are continuously improving.
  - ☐ Run experiments and adapt regularly.
- ☐ **Limit WIP**
  - ☐ Sprint Backlog limits the work for one Sprint.
  - ☐ Maximum of one task per person at a time.
  - ☐ Team works on a limited number of stories at a time.
- ☐ **Minimize lead time**
  - ☐ Sprints are one week (the shorter, the better).
  - ☐ There is no blocked column on a board.
  - ☐ All User Stories are done at the end of the Sprint.

XP PRACTICES CHECKLIST

Scrum is about culture, but you also need to implement development practices from Extreme Programming [36] and focus on software craftsmanship. Here is a checklist of the development practices you will use inside the Scrum process:

- ☐ Continuous integration—several times a day
- ☐ Shared code, collective ownership
- ☐ Coding standards or conventions
- ☐ Test-driven development (TDD)/auto-tests
- ☐ Simple design
- ☐ Pair programming
- ☐ Review
- ☐ Refactoring as a regular activity
- ☐ User Story format

PRODUCT OWNER CHECKLIST

The next area to consider is the checklist of Agile product ownership practices you can suggest to your Product Owner. There are more, but you can start here:

- ☐ Say "no"
- ☐ Product/release charter [37]
- ☐ Story mapping and journey [38]
- ☐ Behavior-driven development (BDD) [39]
- ☐ #NoEstimates [40]
- ☐ Relative weights prioritization [41]
- ☐ Impact mapping [6]
- ☐ Lean start-up [42]

Hints for Great ScrumMasters

- Be aware of the *positivity account statement* and intentionally increase it.
- Mastering takes time; people often need to be years in Shu and years in Ha before entering the Ri stage.
- Root-cause analysis is your best friend. Heal the real disease, not the symptoms.
- Coaching is the most powerful tool you can master. Go to the coaching class and practice. It's worth the effort and money.
- Listen to the voices of the system and believe that everyone is right, though only partially.
- Scaling is not difficult. Do more with LeSS.

8
· · ·
I BELIEVE . . .

I **believe that** anyone can become a great ScrumMaster. Anyone who finds the ScrumMaster's job interesting enough to abandon her current role and position, take the first step into the unknown world of Agile coaching, and is willing to learn this new approach can become a great ScrumMaster.

I **believe that** companies that have such great ScrumMasters have been much more successful than those with traditional hierarchical structures because they are dynamic, creative, and fast learning.

I believe that the great ScrumMaster role is necessary and even crucial for companies' success, regardless of the stage of implementation of Scrum, Agile, Lean, or any other method, process, or way of working.

The Great ScrumMaster

The #ScrumMasterWay is one of the key concepts of this book. The three levels of the great ScrumMaster's development path are crucial to embracing the role on a broader scale. You can't stay at the "My Team" level too long because you might end up as a secretary or just a Scrum guy who becomes unnecessary, your attempts to change anything fruitless and vain. The second level of focusing on Relationships with your team won't stay essential for long either, regardless of how far your management is from Agile people management and how far your project management is from Agile product ownership. Only the last level of Entire System is eye-opening for most ScrumMasters. Only there is the beginning of the path to becoming a great ScrumMaster.

Never forget that the great ScrumMaster is, in the first place, a leader. And as a good leader, she must be self-driven and able to make other people around her successful. Make them flourish. Let them shine.

The great ScrumMaster is a cultural anthropologist. She must be curious about others and have respect for their habits and the way they work. She must be playful and courageous.

Don't Know Whether Agile and Scrum Is for You?

I will facilitate a management workshop to discuss your current issues, understand your particular situation and expectations from such a change, and give you a general introduction to Agile and Scrum.

For general theory you can join my class: Agile and Scrum—Practical Implementation.

Want to Transform Your Organization to Agile?

I will run a workshop to discuss your current situation and suggest the best way to start. Every organization is different and so the approach will differ.

For general theory you can join my class: Agile and Scrum—Transformation and Scaling.

Don't Know How to Build a Good Product Backlog?

During a practical workshop we start with a definition of a good product vision, then create a product charter and, finally, the well-defined User Stories. It's usually a repetitive activity where we periodically go through your Backlog and improve the Backlog Items' quality.

For general theory you can join my class: CSPO—Certified Scrum Product Owner, certified by Scrum Alliance.

Looking for a Way to Improve Your Team?

Agile team coaching is the right approach to choose. It's usually a regular activity when I visit your team once or twice for a Sprint, visit some Scrum events, and coach the ScrumMaster and the team on how to improve.

For general theory you can join my class: CSM—Certified ScrumMaster, certified by Scrum Alliance.

Want to Become a Great ScrumMaster?

Agile and enterprise coaching is the approach I choose in such a situation. I will work with the ScrumMaster on a regular basis to understand the organization's complexity and system thinking.

For general theory you can join my class: CSM—Certified ScrumMaster, certified by Scrum Alliance.

Want to Become a Great Product Owner?

In regular Agile coaching we go through the Product Owner's role, responsibilities, and skills, focusing on the Agile product ownership domain.

For general theory you can join my class: CSPO—Certified Scrum Product Owner certified by Scrum Alliance.

Want to Solve Conflicts?

I use my experience as an ORSC (Organization and Relationship Systems Coaching [4]) coach to improve people's relationships through several coaching sessions/workshops.

Want to Have a Modern Agile Organization?

Through consultancy and enterprise Agile coaching we focus on people development, different leadership styles, and various organization structures.

For general theory you can join my class: Management 3.0.

Want to Move Your Organization to the Next Level?

I use enterprise Agile coaching to support your organization at different levels. It doesn't matter whether you have implemented Agile and Scrum; it's more about searching for better ways of working in general. It's focused on improving teams, collaboration, responsibility, and ownership.

ZUZANA ŠOCHOVÁ—SOCHOVA.COM

I help companies and individuals to be more successful.

I work as an Agile coach and trainer for both large and small organizations. I'm a Certified Scrum Trainer (CST) by Scrum Alliance. I have over 15 years of commercial experience.

Agile Coach

Agile is not only a new methodology, it's a culture that is hard to implement if you haven't experienced it yourself. I have implemented it many times already, in many different companies, so I can help you to implement it in your environment, the way you need it.

Trainer

I love teaching teams and their managers how to be more efficient, how to provide better quality, and how to communicate and organize teams so that people have fun, are motivated, and are highly committed.

I teach both certification classes and regular workshops. All classes are highly interactive and full of hands-on experience.

REFERENCES

[1] James Manktelow and the Mind Tools Team. n.d. "Servant Leadership." www.mindtools.com/pages/article/servant-leadership .htm.

[2] Larry C. Spears. 2010. "Character and Servant Leadership: 10 Characteristics of Effective, Caring Leaders." *The Journal of Virtues and Leadership* 10 (1).

[3] Zuzana Šochová. 2015. "Become a Great ScrumMaster." *Better Software* 17 (4): 30.

[4] Cognitive Edge. n.d. "ORSC: Organization and Relationship Systems Coaching." CRR Global. www.crrglobal.com/organization-relationship-systems-coaching.html.

[5] LeSS Company. 2014. "Systems Thinking." http://less.works/less/principles/systems_thinking.html.

[6] Gojko Adzic. 2012. *Impact Mapping: Making a Big Impact with Software Products and Projects.* Provoking Thoughts.

[7] Gojko Adzic. 2012. "Make a Big Impact with Software Products and Projects!" www.impactmapping.org/.

[8] Cognitive Edge. n.d. "Making Sense of Complexity in Order to Act." http://cognitive-edge.com/.

[9] Julia Wester. 2013. "Understanding the Cynefin Framework—a Basic Intro." Everyday Kanban.

www.everydaykanban.com/2013/09/29/understanding-the-cynefin-framework/.

[10] Agile Coaching Institute. n.d. "Agile Coaching Resources." www.agilecoachinginstitute.com/agile-coaching-resources/.

[11] Eaton & Associates Ltd. 2009. "Tuckman's Model: 5 Stages of Group Development." https://ess110.files.wordpress.com/2009/02/tuckmans_model.pdf.

[12] Patrick Lencioni. 2002. *The Five Dysfunctions of a Team.* Jossey-Bass.

[13] Fernando Lopez. n.d. "The Top 4 Behaviors That Doom Relationships—and What to Do about Them." www.orscglobal.com/MainCommunity/Resources/Top4BehaviorsThatDoomRelationships.pdf.

[14] Christopher Avery. n.d. "Christopher Avery—The Responsibility Process." www.christopheravery.com/.

[15] Dave Logan, John King, and Halee Fischer-Wright. 2011. *Tribal Leadership: Leveraging Natural Groups to Build a Thriving Organization.* HarperBusiness.

[16] David Marquet. 2013. *Turn the Ship Around!: A True Story of Turning Followers into Leaders.* Portfolio.

[17] LeSS Company. n.d. "Sprint Review." http://less.works/less/framework/sprint-review.html.

[18] Mindview. n.d. "What Is an OpenSpace Conference?" www.mindviewinc.com/Conferences/OpenSpaces.

[19] Wikipedia. n.d. "Unconference." https://en.wikipedia.org/wiki/Unconference.

[20] World Café. n.d. "World Cafe Method." www.theworldcafe.com/key-concepts-resources/world-cafe-method/.

[21] CRR Global. n.d. "ORSC Intelligence: A Roadmap for Change." www.crrglobal.com/intelligence.html.

[22] John Kotter. 2006. *Our Iceberg Is Melting: Changing and Succeeding under Any Conditions.* Macmillan.

[23] Alistair Cockburn. 2008. "Shu Ha Ri." http://alistair.cockburn .us/Shu+Ha+Ri.

[24] Francis Takahashi. 2012. "An Interview with Endô Seishirô Shihan by Aiki News." www.aikidoacademyusa.com/viewtopic .php?f=14&t=336#p545.

[25] Cognitive Edge. 2011. "ORSC: Organization and Relationship Systems Coaching—Coach Training Courses." CRR Global. www.crrglobal.com/coach-training-courses .html.

[26] Marcial Losada and Emily Heaphy. 2014. "The Role of Positivity and Connectivity in the Performance of Business Teams: A Nonlinear Dynamics Model." www.scuoladipaloalto .it/wp-content/uploads/2012/11/positive-to-negative-attractors-in-business-teams11.pdf.

[27] Amit Amin. 2014. "The Power of Positivity, in Moderation: The Losada Ratio." http://happierhuman.com/losada-ratio/.

[28] Amit Amin. 2014. "The Power and Vestigiality of Positive Emotion—What's Your Happiness Ratio?" http://happierhuman .com/positivity-ratio/.

[29] John Whitmore. 2009. *Coaching for Performance: GROWing Human Potential and Purpose.* Nicholas Brealey Publishing.

[30] International Coach Federation (ICF). n.d. "Code of Ethics—About—ICF." http://coachfederation.org/about/ ethics.aspx?ItemNumber=854.

[31] Henry Kimsey-House, Karen Kimsey-House, and Phillip Sandahl. 2011. "Powerful Questions." www.thecoaches.com/ docs/resources/toolkit/pdfs/31-Powerful-Questions.pdf.

[32] Agile Coaching Institute. 2011. "Powerful Questions Cards from the Coaching Agile Teams Class." www.agilecoachinginstitute .com/wp-content/uploads/2011/05/PQ-Cards-4-to-a-page.pdf.

[33] Gojko Adzic. 2012. "Make a Big Impact with Software Products and Projects!" www.impactmapping.org/about.php.

[34] LeSS Company. 2014. "Large-Scale Scrum—LeSS." http://less.works/.

[35] LeSS Company. 2014. "LeSS Case Studies." http://less.works/case-studies/index.html.

[36] Don Wells. 1999. "The Rules of Extreme Programming." www.extremeprogramming.org/rules.html.

[37] Michael Lant. 2010. "How to Make Your Project Not Suck by Using an Agile Project Charter." http://michaellant.com/2010/05/18/how-to-make-your-project-not-suck/.

[38] Jeff Patton. 2008. "The New User Story Backlog Is a Map." http://jpattonassociates.com/the-new-backlog/.

[39] Agile Alliance. 2013. "BDD." http://guide.agilealliance.org/guide/bdd.html.

[40] Vasco Duarte. 2014. "5 No Estimates Decision-Making Strategies." http://noestimatesbook.com/blog/.

[41] Zuzi Šochová. 2013. "Forgotten Practices: The Backlog Priority Game." http://tulming.com/agile-and-lean/forgotten-practices-the-backlog-priority-game/.

[42] Eric Ries. n.d. "The Lean Startup Methodology." http://theleanstartup.com/principles.

INDEX

A

Absence of trust, as team dysfunction, 66

Abstract skills. *See* Metaskills

Accountability
dysfunctional teams avoiding, 67
ScrumMaster role in dysfunctional team, 68
for toxic behavior, 71

Actors, in impact mapping, 116, 118

Agile
assessing your competency in, 58–59
finding out if it is for you, 126
Practical Implementation class, 126
ScrumMaster must be expert in, 2, 7, 54–55
staying one step ahead in changeover to, 16–17
teaching/mentoring when starting, 24–25
Transformation and Scaling class, 127
transforming organization into, 127

Agile wheel, 88–90

B

Best practices, in Cynefin framework, 47

Blame
laying, 73
as team toxin, 69, 71

Blog posts, as resources for ScrumMasters, 54–55

Book club, decentralizing teams via, 85

Brainstorming, in meetings, 108, 109

Bright side, increasing positivity by looking at, 105

Business knowledge, core competency in, 57–59

Buy-in, to change, 93

C

Certified Scrum Master (CSM), 127

Certified Scrum Product Owner (CSPO), 127, 128

Change management
assessing competency in, 58–59
change behavior, 90–91
clarifying using Agile Wheel, 88–89
as core competency, 57
difficulty of implementing, 87
in Entire System level of #ScrumMasterWay, 37
focus on system view, 44–46
ScrumMaster as team member and, 10

REGISTER YOUR PRODUCT at informit.com/register
Access Additional Benefits and SAVE 35% on Your Next Purchase

- Download available product updates.

- Access bonus material when applicable.

- Receive exclusive offers on new editions and related products.
  (Just check the box to hear from us when setting up your account.)

- Get a coupon for 35% for your next purchase, valid for 30 days. Your code will
  be available in your InformIT cart. (You will also find it in the Manage Codes
  section of your account page.)

Registration benefits vary by product. Benefits will be listed on your account page
under Registered Products.

InformIT.com–The Trusted Technology Learning Source
InformIT is the online home of information technology brands at Pearson, the world's foremost
education company. At InformIT.com you can
- Shop our books, eBooks, software, and video training.
- Take advantage of our special offers and promotions (informit.com/promotions).
- Sign up for special offers and content newsletters (informit.com/newsletters).
- Read free articles and blogs by information technology experts.
- Access thousands of free chapters and video lessons.

Connect with InformIT–Visit informit.com/community
Learn about InformIT community events and programs.

the trusted technology learning source

Addison-Wesley · Cisco Press · IBM Press · Microsoft Press · Pearson IT Certification · Prentice Hall · Que · Sams · VMware Press